Never Too Late to Dream

The 1994 Chapel of the Air 50-Day Spiritual Adventure
"Daring to Dream Again"

Never Too Late to Dream, by David Mains. Discover how to break through the barriers of your past and prejudices, your self-centeredness and anxieties, and reclaim the dreams God has planted in your heart. Book includes group discussion questions. Catalog no. 6-3203.

Back to Your Spiritual Future, by Steve Bell. As the author remembers the highs and lows of his own continuing spiritual journey, he also shares biblical principles and insights to help you refocus your priorities and get back to your spiritual future. Includes individual and group work sections. Catalog no. 6-3205.

How to Be a World-Class Christian, by Paul Borthwick. You can be a part of God's global action—from your own neighborhood to the "ends of the earth." Special 50-Day Adventure abridged edition. Catalog no. 6-3204.

Adventure Journals. Dig deeper into the adventure with day-by-day personal growth exercises. Available in the following editions:

Adult	Catalog no. 6-8830
Student	Catalog no. 6-8832
Children, grades 3–6	Catalog no. 6-8831
Critter County Activity Book	Catalog no. 6-8833

ALSO AVAILABLE

Church Starter Kit	Catalog no. 6-8838
Children's Church Leader's Guide	
	Catalog no. 6-8836
Small Group Starter Kit	Catalog no. 6-8839
Student Leader's Guide	Catalog no. 6-8828

NEVER TOO LATE TO
DREAM

David Mains

VICTOR BOOKS

A DIVISION OF SCRIPTURE PRESS PUBLICATIONS INC.
USA CANADA ENGLAND

Copyediting: Barbara Williams
Cover Design: Scott Rattray
Cover Illustration: Tony Stone Images

ISBN: 1-56476-203-3

1   2   3   4   5   6   7   8   9   10   Printing/Year   97   96   95   94   93

CONTENTS

I want to express my appreciation to Chariot Family Publishing for allowing me to quote extensively from *Tales of the Resistance*. I would also like to dedicate this book to Cathy Davis, Executive Editor, for her help.

In the chapters that follow, you will get acquainted with some of the characters in the *Tales*. These will whet your appetite to meet others who appear in both the *Tales of the Kingdom* and the *Tales of the Resistance*.

In choosing the fictional personalities I have, I'm sorry you don't get to know:

> The Carnival Daughter
> The Sewer Rat and the Boiler Brat
> The Girl Named "Dirty"
> The Baker Who Loved Bread
> The Two Noisy Knights
> The Apprentice Juggler
> The Faithless Ranger
> and many more

These tales were written for children of all ages. Like all good stories, they teach lessons of great value.

INTRODUCTION

How did I get myself into this? I mused as I got dressed that Monday morning several years back. *My schedule for this week is already too full. Why did I agree to take a whole day to talk with an industrial psychologist?*

Then I remembered. A Chapel of the Air board member had suggested this meeting. That's what it was. He knew a professional who had offered his services free of charge to several executives of Christian ministries. This psychologist had said he would be glad to give a day of his time to talk with those leaders about their dreams. Possibly he could be of help in seeing their visions find fulfillment. For him that would be a way to use his gifts in the Lord's work. But no one took him up on his offer. "Would you be interested?" my board member wanted to know. He could arrange a meeting.

What was I to say? At the time, our broadcast was struggling. The board wasn't confident we would make it. The reasons are too complex to go into. But as a staff we had cut back our already thin work force. Now all of us had more to do than we could handle. Looking back on that time, I recall it was like trying to outrun a bullet. Could we race fast enough ... and for long enough? We might make it. Might! ... but the odds weren't good.

This is ridiculous, I thought as I drove to where we would be meeting. *I don't have time for dreams anymore. My present ministry has gone about as far as it's ever going to go. My visions seem to have come to an abrupt halt. End of the line, buddy! Face it, David, you don't have the luxury of dreaming.*

Our meeting was at a private Chicago club. I wasn't paying—the psychologist I hadn't yet met was. The conference room was large and luxurious, quite a contrast to the setting of the staff get-together I had held the Friday before. Around the table in our small lunchroom I had outlined to my key workers the financial status of the "Chapel." We had coffee, but not served from a silver pot. Now in this new setting four of us sat around a gorgeous table that could comfortably accommodate a dozen. A tray of sweets came with the coffee service. Then the gentleman who had invited me took over and explained the agenda to me, to my board member, and to one of my top executives.

"It's my privilege to have you as guests. I want very much to use my gifts on behalf of the Lord. But sometimes at church it seems my only choices are ushering, teaching a junior high class, or singing in the choir. My best skills relate to working with executives. So again, thank you for allowing me to see if I can be of help."

I warmed to his approach and soon felt at ease. Then as he continued I heard an expression I didn't understand. "Hopefully," he said, "we'll break glass before long. That's one of my desires."

"Break glass," I stopped him, "I don't know what that means."

"Most people don't see their dreams fulfilled, their visions become reality, because their thinking has become restricted," he explained. "It's like being in a great room such as this one, only with a glass ceiling overhead. You can see above you, but you can't get into that new horizon unless you break the glass ceiling and open up for yourself that greater world."

"Will I know when that happens?" I questioned.

"You'll know when we get to such a place," he responded. "Then you'll have to decide what to do. Hopefully we can break glass a couple of times today. That's one of the gifts I can give you. But first, tell me what the Lord has called you to do, David. What's He laid on your heart? What are His dreams for you?"

Now it was my turn to talk. But it wasn't as easy as I had thought. Again, I wasn't in a dreaming mood. We were operating with a "survive another week" mind-set. My ministry world was shutting down, not expanding. Still, I tried to put the immediate aside and talk about what the Lord had laid on my heart in the earlier days of my ministry. Mostly that related to seeing the church come alive.

Words came out about our being a ministry that was a servant to the church, that encouraged pastors, that helped laypeople discover and use their gifts even as this man wanted to do. As a ministry we dared to believe that Christians cared deeply about seeing another great spiritual awakening—a revival of faith that would begin in individual lives and then affect marriages, enhance family relationships, touch the workplace, build up our churches, beautify our cities, and make our nation strong in every way.

As time passed, I told my host about our annual 50-Day Spiritual Adventures, how they were tools for accelerated spiritual growth, that those who participated could measure their progress, and how the number of individuals and churches involved had grown year by year.

"Are your Adventure materials offered overseas?" he asked.

"To a limited degree," I replied. "We've done extensive experiments in India with over a hundred thousand participants. The materials have been translated into Spanish and also tested in. . . ."

"I would think they could be even more effective overseas than they are here," he postured. "From my observations, missions organizations are better at evangelism than they are at discipleship. Your Adventure journals would be perfect in places like Nigeria, the Philippines, Honduras. . . ."

"But you don't understand," I interrupted. "We're scrambling just to make it in North America. The cost of purchasing airtime is very high. Over half the Christian programmers on the air don't pay for their time on many of the commercial stations, but the Chapel does. Listeners don't know that. We struggle to meet budget. I don't have the luxury of talking about overseas projects. It's hard enough. . . ."

"Hold on," the psychologist said loudly. "I believe we have just come to a glass-breaking time. You agree there's a great need for materials like these overseas, but your mind is conditioned to go only so far. Then it bumps into a ceiling of your own making. You're not dreaming new possibilities because you're accustomed to a ceiling where it is now. The question is whether you're willing to break glass so we can at least *explore* various options and their ramifications."

It's amazing that even now as I write, I can still feel the tension of that moment. *Why take time to explore what isn't reality?* I questioned. *This new territory is out of bounds for me.*

My host didn't give up. He reasoned, "Maybe the overseas market is the key to future growth for you."

I didn't want to hear that.

"Maybe overseas expansion could resolve your money problems," he continued.

I knew it wouldn't. Missions projects only added to the expense column.

"Can we at least talk about it?" he wondered.

Silence.

"Well, now, are we going to break glass or aren't we?"

"OK," I finally acquiesced. "Let's go for it."

An hour and a half later we were at another "glass-breaking" juncture, another ceiling to be shattered, and another jumbling up of all my familiar thought patterns.

Finally it was lunchtime. Thank the Lord! I'd try to get my head reoriented and think through the ramifications of what was being discussed.

Half an hour after lunch we came to another glass ceiling that needed to be shattered. *So why not,* I thought, *let's bust it out!*

But fifteen minutes later I had a headache built for a rhinoceros!

"I need to stop," I confessed. "My normal thinking circuits are so hopelessly rewired I can't function without great strain."

"Then I suggest we quit," the psychologist said. "This has been a good day. I believe I've given you a great gift. It happened faster than I thought it would. So I'm pleased.

Again, thank you for letting me exercise my gift."

I'm glad I've made him so happy, I thought, recognizing the irony in the situation.

But looking back on that meeting, I realize it was one of the best things that ever happened to me. I've been involved in a lot of brainstorming sessions, but this one literally changed my life.

In the ensuing months and years our ministry went through an amazing turnaround. And best of all, now I'm dreaming again. Not my dreams—I believe they're the Lord's dreams for me.

Taking a cue from my own experience, I think a large percentage of Christians have glass ceilings that need to be shattered. I suspect this is so because their faith appears to be suffocated. They function with less spiritual breathing room than they used to. Once they had dreams of what their lives could mean for God, but somewhere along the line those dreams died. How sad. Maybe you can identify with believers like that.

The problem is not something new to this generation. For example, Scripture tells us Gideon had a similar experience. When the angel of the Lord first appeared, he greeted Gideon with these positive words, "The Lord is with you, mighty warrior" (Jud. 6:12).

According to Judges 6:13, Gideon replied, "But sir . . . if the Lord is with us, why has all this happened to us?" Gideon was referring to the oppression of the Jews by the Midianites. That's why Gideon questioned, "Where are all His wonders that our fathers told us about when they said, 'Did not the Lord bring us up out of Egypt?' But now the Lord has abandoned us and put us into the hand of Midian."

Gideon wasn't exactly in a dreaming mood, either. But in the encounter that followed, some glass ceilings were broken right there near the winepress where he had been threshing wheat. And when Gideon said in essence, "God, I want Your dreams for me to be my dreams as well," it was a new and a wonderful day for Israel.

That's what I want for myself and for you, that we dare to dream again. It's never too late to dream God's dreams for us. We can break through the barriers that hold us back and become—in this opportune time when God pours out His Spirit—those sons and daughters who prophesy, those older folks who dream dreams, and that younger generation which can still embrace visions (Joel 2:28).

CHAPTER ONE

LET GO OF OUR PAINFUL PAST

Hero was afraid.

He watched the Ranger hold a burning torch to the ring of stones that circled the place of the Great Celebration. The Sacred Flames ignited with a w-o-o-O-O-O-SH, lifting the hems of the blue robes of the protectors of Great Park, who stood as sentries around Inmost Circle. The silver insignia of the Rangers caught the light and flashed in the outer circle around the rim of fire.

Tonight he would leave these friends, leave Mercie and Caretaker, leave these woods, these dear fields, leave everything in the world he had come to love. Well, *almost everything,* he reminded himself: What he loved most in the world was the King and to be a King's man and to do the King's work.

And the voice of that King, the most beautiful of men, had spoken inwardly only this morning: *It is time. It is time to begin the restoration of the Kingdom. I need a King's man with a hero's heart. Will you come?*

This is how my wife, Karen, and I begin the Gold Medallion Award-winning book, *Tales of the Resistance.* It's written for children of all ages to enjoy. I'll use sections from these tales to develop the themes of the chapters which follow in this book.

Far off, Ranger horns sounded from the watchtowers that guarded Deepest Forest. *Croi-croi!* Come-come! *Croi-Croi!* Come to Inmost Circle! Come to the solemn assembly!

Hero watched as the people he loved made entrance, passed through the Sacred Flames and became real. He watched Amanda step into the fire a ragtag tomboy and step out a beautiful, graceful princess. He watched the unhappy woman who had been the orphan keeper's assistant become someone with a mother's smile for all the children, who ran to hug her. He saw Caretaker become Ranger Commander.

How can I ever go? thought Hero. *How can I leave all this?* But he had heard the voice of his King: *Come, Hero. It is time. And he knew he must go.*

A Dream in Your Heart

Like young Hero in this tale, I assume you know a little of what it's like to have the King place a dream in your heart. And not just any dream—His dream. Being able to dream God's dreams for us is a marvelous privilege.

This is not the same as personal dreams for a bigger house . . . a better job . . . more acclaim. God's dreams for us involve service—valorous service on behalf of His Majesty.

What dreams has God placed in your heart?

* Maybe you were first in your family to meet the King, and you dreamed of sharing this experience with all those you loved. Or . . .

* You dreamed of studying the Bible and someday being able to share its marvelous truths with people in need. You could picture yourself giving of your faith and delighting the Lord with your love for Him. Or . . .

* You dreamed of starting a youth group where "King's love" could be experienced by guys and girls who were looking for it in all the wrong places. Or . . .

* You dreamed about helping plant a church in a growing subdivision where you purchased a new house. Or . . .

* You wanted to establish a new congregation in the inner city. I dreamed that dream once. In my mind I could see a

church of whites and blacks, Hispanics and Asian Americans, all worshiping together, modeling the oneness in the body that Christ prayed for.

* Maybe your dreams concerned another country. Your aspirations might have been so expansive that they required others to work alongside you.

How have you responded to the dreams God has given you? Perhaps you've felt the way Hero did as he anticipated going forth to serve the King:

... This solemn assembly had been hurriedly gathered for the Rite of Adoption, for no lad could go back into Enchanted City an orphan. Orphans belonged to the evil Enchanter. Hero must be someone's son; he must have proof of parentage to protect him.

Dread filled his soul. He thought of the darkness of Enchanted City, where the citizens worked by night and slept by day. He remembered Burning Place where the dead were burned: all who had died of weariness, of hunger, of heartsickness.

In his memory, he saw fire burning the pyre that held his mother's body. (She had always said, "There is a King. A real King!") Death drums began to beat in his mind: *oo-mb-pha ... oo-mb-pha ... oo-mb-pha-din.* Visions of Burners with hot brands and smoldering pokers flashed. He heard the blows of the Breakers. The song of the Naysayers, *nay-nay-nay, nay-nay-nay, nay-nay-nay,* clutched his heart with icy fingers.

He remembered Branding—himself a screaming five-year-old—and how the hot iron had seared his cheek. For the first time in many months, Hero touched the scar. Here, in this place among these people, he was Hero, loved by many. In that terrible place, he was nothing but scum. The people of Enchanted City would point and jeer in the old way—Scarboy! Scarboy!

S-C-A-R-B-O-Y!!

Suddenly, Hero heard a scream rise out of Enchanted City and fall into a paralyzing moan in his own soul. He raised up his head, startled. It was more than memory.

Hero knew it was the voice of the evil Enchanter from the dark midst of the Dagoda, with his fiery head thrown back, with fire priests dancing and their ceremonial bells jangling: *jchang-jchang-jchang.*

S-C-A-R-B-O-Y!!

Hero cowered, standing outside the Circle of Flames. His heart felt like stone. The hot eye of the Enchanter had found him, here in his fear. How could he follow the King if he kept hearing this loud and terrible cry? He would be vulnerable, alone.

"Oh, Mercie," the lad whispered to the old, old woman beside him. "I'm afraid. How will I ever find the King? You know I'm not good at recognizing disguises. I can *feel* the Enchanter's hot eye, and hear the *nay-din-nay-din* of Enchanted City, and remember the brands and the blows and the stink of Burning Place."

The old woman took his hand, and Hero felt the strength of her grasp. Mercie smiled. "Hero, fear is ever the Enchanter's ally. Have you forgotten your own powerful weapons?"

A painful past can often inhibit our dreams. Perhaps you've experienced pain such as . . .

* A split of close friends within a church
* The failure of a spiritual leader you trusted
* Betrayal by a Christian friend you went to for help, who told others about your problem
* An experience where you tried your best to serve the Lord, but you failed
* Embarrassment by a harsh authority figure
* Criticism from class members you were teaching
* Having your best efforts sabotaged by a ruling board
* Being left for another by your mate
* Horrible memories of childhood abuse just now starting to surface

For me, after feeling I had failed in my inner city efforts, I was afraid to open myself to dreaming again for well over a decade. I ministered assuming something bad would happen that would undermine whatever I tried to do. My leadership style was careful and guarded. But I found in time that it wasn't nearly as much fun serving the Lord like that. I still wanted to believe He had a dream for me that fit perfectly into what He was doing in His world.

Maybe that's how you feel. A cacophony of voices from your past screams in your mind, "Your real name is Scarboy ... or Scargirl. You'll never make it when it comes to serving this King of yours!"

If we're not careful, we adopt the names others give us and forget that God calls us to be heroes, that in His eyes we are not destined to be frightened but instead are meant to be men and women of valor.

"Come on, David," you say. "It's a tale for children you're referring to, remember? This is the real world, not Great Park and Enchanted City."

Born to Be a Hero

Then let me review briefly a tale you know about another young man born to be a hero. He knew instinctively that this was so. In fact, he tried his own hand at doing a mighty work for the Lord, righting a grievous wrong, establishing himself as a champion for God. Touched by the injustice he saw, he actually slew an oppressor of his people, and by doing so he became a marked man for life. There might as well have been a scar on his cheek too! Everyone knew him on sight, except maybe those at some far edge of the world. So that's where he fled and subsequently stayed for forty-some years. That's until the Lord came and said, "You don't know who you are, Moses. You were born to be one of My early heroes."

Not ready to break the glass ceiling of his limited thinking, Moses protested (Ex. 3:11), "Who am I, that I should go to Pharaoh and bring the Israelites out of Egypt? [Why, I bet my picture is still up in every post office in Egypt!]"

(Ex. 4:1): "What if they do not believe me or listen to me and say, 'The Lord did not appear to you'? [It's going to sound stupid when I explain that You talked to me through a bush that was on fire!]"

(Ex. 4:10): "O Lord, I have never been eloquent, neither in

the past nor since You have spoken to Your servant. I am slow of speech and tongue. [I-I ge-get ti-ti-tired of p-p-people saying 'Eh?' and 'What?']"

(Ex. 4:13): "O Lord, [pa-pa] please send someone else to do it."

Moses didn't use the words "I have a painful past." But he might just as well have, because going back to the Enchanted City in Egypt was the last thing he wanted to do.

Listen, Moses, dreaming God's dreams for us often requires letting go of painful past experiences.

I've had to say those words to myself: "Listen, David Mains, dreaming God's dreams for us often requires letting go of painful past experiences."

And I repeat the words for you, whatever your name is. Dreaming God's dreams for us often requires letting go of painful past experiences.

Do you identify at all with the words of this prayer:

Lord,
Daring to dream again sounds so good,
   But sometimes memories of broken dreams haunt me.
Help me let go of the pain
That keeps me from responding to Your gentle nudgings.
Your presence encourages me to set aside fear
   And to become a spiritual risk-taker.
I want Your dreams for me to be my dreams as well.
AMEN

If this prayer had been written in Moses' day, he might well have resonated with it. At first it appeared he had no intention of coming out of hiding—of daring to dream again. That left a question to be answered. How then could the people of God be delivered from their oppression?

The answer is that Moses needed to be healed of painful memories in order to do his divinely assigned job. He would have to learn to break through this barrier that held him back. The Lord needed to help His servant let go of the hurt of his past. Fortunately, that's God's speciality, isn't it—healing broken people.

God would gently nudge Moses into action. His yet-to-be hero dared not live with a "forever victim" mentality. Sooner or later the "spiritual hero" side of all of us should begin to emerge also. That can happen as the church, which needs to be more than a ward for the walking wounded, points the way to healing and helps us move forward.

If this doesn't happen, we are a sad bunch indeed. We can't be part of the Lord's magnificent dream for this world if we are held back by painful memories.

Incidentally, the people of God held captive in Egypt were delivered. Moses was able to let go of the past. He truly did play the hero. And aren't we glad?

Let's return to our young fictional Hero. He has heard the voice of his King speak in his heart that it is time to return to Enchanted City to begin the restoration of the kingdom. Painful memories from childhood, including the fact that he was called Scarboy, make this a hard assignment for him to accept—just like Moses.

"Ranger initiate!" called out Commander. "Stand forth for Revealing!"

With a pounding heart, Hero obeyed. He had always longed to be a Ranger, a protector of Great Park, but never, never had he felt so unworthy as at this moment.

Kneeling and bowing, Hero felt Ranger Commander's hand placed firmly on his head. The voice which always filled him with awe spoke above him.

"Tonight we are gathered to induct the lad Hero into the corps of Rangers, protectors and watchkeepers for the King. What is your pleasure?"

The blue-cloaked men and women spoke as one: "Let the ceremony begin!"

The awful first question was asked: "Does anyone know just cause why this one, Hero, should not be invested with the office of Ranger?"

Each Ranger in the circle answered in turn.

"I do not," said the first.

"Nor do I," called out the next.

The lad kneeled in an agony of suspense. He longed

with all his being for this office, but he wished someone would speak to his unworthiness before he shamed them all by being a faithless Ranger.

"Nor I—nor I." And so, round the circle came the pledges of faith. Hero could hardly believe that not one Ranger would show just cause that he was unworthy.

Then the second awful question: "Do you, initiate, hold just cause against yourself?"

Hero sighed deeply. Revealing demanded honesty. Lifting his head, he looked into Commander's eyes, "Sire, I—I am afraid. I am afraid of the task at hand."

A murmur went up from the blue-cloaked circle. A voice cried, "No just cause! Even the most courageous fear the unknown task!"

Hero gulped. "But Sire, I—I doubt. The mettle of the powers is unknown to me. I fear its weakness against the force of Enchanted City."

Another voice cried, "Power is always untested until it has been tried. No just cause!"

Hero spoke one last time. "Sire, my seeing is dim, and the voice of the Enchanter is near."

Ranger Commander answered, "Dim sight is cured by choosing to see. We hear the voice of whomever we allow near. No just cause. Stand forth!"

Hero rose from his knees. Ranger Commander called above his head, "What is the pleasure of this company? Shall we induct this Hero, once of Enchanted City, now of Great Park, for the task at hand?"

A hurrah went up from the circle of Rangers, followed by another larger shout from the crowd standing beyond. "To vows! To vows!"

Hero's heart swelled with this honor. He would be a Ranger. He would fight for the King. He would give his forever pledge to protect the Kingdom, to be faithful. "To the King!" he shouted.

"To the King!" all shouted back.

"To the Restoration!"

The kingdom—that's the big picture too many in the

church have lost sight of today. It was Christ's key message. He talked about the kingdom again and again, His present and future kingdom.

Christ's kingdom, or kingship, is wherever He is recognized as King, His will is obeyed, and subjects reap the benefit of His rule.

Heaven is that way. All subjects there bow before Christ as King. In heaven all are obedient to His will and reap great benefits. So heaven is the kingdom, or kingship, of Christ.

But the kingdom is here as well. When we bow to Christ as Lord and obey His will, we are the ones who benefit as we live under His gracious kingship. In fact, Christ taught us to pray, "Your kingdom come, Your will be done on earth as it is in heaven" (Matt. 6:10).

Kingdom people believe in restoration—in release from oppression in Egypt and even worse settings. It is the King's ultimate dream for the world that we cherish.

Now is the time to again dream great dreams for our Lord. His return may be soon. Can we be King's men and King's women in this day? Can we put the pain of our past experiences aside? It is important to recognize that:

* The person who hurt you may never ask forgiveness.
* The marvelous ministry job you did may never be recognized.
* Some injustices may never be righted.
* The sin committed against you could go unconfessed to the grave!

But for the sake of the future, you can still say, "I'll put past hurts and fears aside. I want to hear once again the call of my King. With Christ it's never too late to dream."

I want your story to be like the story of Hero in the tale I've been sharing.

"Now," said Mercie beside him, "the Rites of Adoption." The beautiful woman pressed two fingers to Hero's forehead. She steadied the back of his head with her other hand. The Rangers in the near circle lifted their hatchets, blades pointed toward him, and a hum, one note only, began.

"I, wife of Caretaker, war-maiden Ranger, do implant you, Ranger Hero, with this proof of parentage. You will always know you belong to us. You are ours. Orphan no more, you are heir to all we hold."

Hero closed his eyes and listened to the simple one-note hum. The place on his forehead which Mercie touched grew warm; then the gentle warmth diffused through his whole body. It was only when he opened his eyes that he realized every hatchet had been sheathed and that the hum he heard, the one-note hum, was now in his own brain, in his own ears, in his own heart.

The people of Great Park began to leave; wordlessly, they withdrew into Deepest Forest. Amanda gave him a shy hug. Her eyes glistened with tears. On the edge of the crowd, special friends waved silent farewells. Each Ranger clasped his hand and then departed. The Sacred Flames dimmed and died, leaving only glowing charcoals to mark the circle.

Hero stood alone with Caretaker and old Mercie.

"It is time," said Caretaker. "We will accompany you as far as Burning Place."

So the three walked together out of Inmost Circle, through Deepest Forest, past the practice field, deserted in the night, along the path by Caretaker's cottage where the latest outcasts rested in sleep, down the edge of wildflower Woods to the old stone gates of Great Park.

A faint melon-wedge of light cracked the night sky, and Hero realized he would leave Great Park at the same time of day, dawn, that he had once entered it so many seasons ago.

Caretaker raised his hatchet and the familiar hymn-hum began. The gates creaked open slowly, and the three walked beneath the inscription: WELCOME ALL WHO HUNT.

Hero turned and watched the gates close behind him. "Will I ever see this place again?" he wondered out loud.

Mercie pulled him around to face Enchanted City. "Nonsense," she snapped. "You'll see it every time you close your eyes." Little as she was, she was now without pity and her grasp was mighty on his arm.

The two old people walked on either side of the boy. Hero dragged his heavy feet through the garbage dump, filled with rotten refuse, which separated Great Park from Enchanted City. Closer they came, closer and closer to Burning Place, just outside the city walls. And all the while, Hero sensed that Mercie and Caretaker were growing fainter, dimming somehow here in the rank air that smelled of smoke and fire. They were fading away from him. In the soft light, Hero read a sign which proclaimed:

THERE IS NO SUCH THING AS A KING. DEATH TO PRETENDERS!

His feet kicked the soft ashes, and Hero knew he had finally returned, come back to the one place that he hated above all others.

"Mercie," he whispered. "Caretaker?"

They were gone.

They had left him here on the edge of Burning Place, alone, without aid. Abandoned. Helpless. Unloved. No, no wait. Hero took a deep breath.

He closed his eyes and thought back to where he had just been. Inmost Circle. Within the leaping Sacred Flames. He remembered the cry, "To vows!" and recalled the strong pulse of life clasped in the Ranger grasp. He was not alone. He might be on the edge of the evil Enchanted City, but wonderful things had happened to him. He belonged to somebody. He was loved.

At that moment, with his eyes still closed, he heard the lovely hum. It was not just a memory out of the past. It was with him now, in his ears, in his own brain. As Hero listened, the flailing in his heart was quieted. The hum grew from one note to many, and from many notes to the full music of Great Celebration.

And there in the light of dawn, of a new day, as the people of the city ended their work and prepared to sleep, Hero lifted his head and held forth his arms. His back straightened, Ranger tall, and he began the dance, kicking the ashes of Burning Place as he stepped to the glorious chords of the inward melody. And for those who were still awake to hear, a laugh, young and joyous, rose from outside the walls and settled in the morning air.

For the lad, Hero, discovered that when one belongs to the Kingdom, he is never alone in the terrible places of the world; he can always hear the single, clear-note hum.

FOR DISCUSSION AND REFLECTION

1. Have you recently heard someone in a conversation give evidence of holding on to a painful past experience? How common a problem do you think this is?

2. Why do painful past experiences often inhibit people from dreaming God's dreams for themselves or for the church?

3. Almost everyone has had a negative church experience of one kind or another. What is a memory like this which you might do well to put behind you?

4. Do you, like Moses, have any memories of trying to serve the Lord and being hurt in the process?

5. If a person said, "I don't know how to put memories like this behind me," what advice would you offer?

6. How good does "daring to dream again" sound to you?

READINGS

I doubt we can ever put our pasts *behind* us when we've never put them *before* us. Yet many of us stall on the starting line of change because we fear that we'll lose family members' approval and affection.

I once counseled with a charming thirty-something Christian who grew up in a subtly, but profoundly, unhealthy home. She said her birth family's motto was "family first." I think that meant, "Ignore and don't talk about who and what's hurtful in this family." An alternative translation might be: "Don't rock the boat (with truth) even if it's the Titanic!"

We will never begin the move from hurting to healing until we answer the question: "Whose rules rule?" The person whose rules we are living by is god to us! If, in an attempt to gain the parental seal of approval, we continue to live by the rules of hurting, hurtful parents, we will continue our hurting, hurtful ways. But if we choose to know God and put him on the throne of our lives, we will begin to live by His rules. And, as we've already seen, God takes truth very seriously.

I read somewhere that calling a thing by its correct name is the beginning of change. Some of us will need to begin calling our family loyalty *lying,* if that is its correct name. Yet, just contemplating such a genuinely truth-based approach to our entire lives, we may feel as alien in our families as salmon would be in the Sahara! Yet God and commitment to change call us to begin dealing honestly with our pasts as well as our present lives. We must face the pain inherent in becoming truth-tellers in truth-fearing families. We are foolish to expect reality-phobic family members to jump up, click their heels together, and exclaim, "Oh, goody goody. We've all been wondering when someone would get healthy enough to start changing so that we'd be confronted with our personal and family dysfunction and be dragged kicking and screaming into greater wholeness!" It just doesn't work that way.

In unhealthy systems, whether they're families or companies, the person who sees and speaks the problem becomes the problem. Instead of working to resolve the problem, such systems focus on removing the problem-perceiver.

Hurt People Hurt People, Sandra D. Wilson, Thomas Nelson, pages 94–95.

■　■　■

Through fifteen years, as tapes have gone out all over the world, letters and testimonies have confirmed my belief that there is another realm of problems which requires a special kind of prayer and a deeper level of healing by the Spirit. Somewhere between our sins, on the one hand, and our sicknesses, on the other, lies an area the Scripture calls "infirmities."

We can explain this by an illustration from nature. If you visit the far West, you will see those beautiful giant sequoia and redwood trees. In most of the parks the naturalists can show you a cross section of a great tree they have cut, and point out that the rings of the tree reveal the developmental history, year by year. Here's a ring that represents a year when there was a terrible drought. Here are a couple of rings from years when there was too much rain. Here's where the tree was struck by lightning. Here are some normal years of growth. This rings shows a forest fire that almost destroyed the tree. Here's another of savage blight and disease. All of this lies embedded in the heart of the tree, representing the autobiography of its growth.

And that's the way it is with us. Just a few minutes beneath the protective bark, the concealing, protective mask, are the recorded rings of our lives.

There are scars of ancient, painful hurts . . . as when a little boy rushed downstairs one Christmas dawn and discovered in his Christmas stocking a dirty old rock, put there to punish him for some trivial boyhood naughtiness. This scar has eaten away in him, causing all kinds of interpersonal difficulties.

Here is the discoloration of a tragic stain that muddied all of life . . . as years ago behind the barn, or in the haystack, or out in the woods, a big brother took a little sister and introduced her into the mysteries—no, the miseries of sex.

And here we see the pressure of a painful, repressed memory . . . of running after an alcoholic father who was about to kill the mother, and then of rushing for the butcher knife. Such scars have been buried in pain for so long that they are causing hurt and rage that are inexplicable. And these scars are not touched by conversion and sanctifying grace, or by the ordinary benefits of prayer.

In the rings of our thoughts and emotions, the record is there; the memories are recorded, and all are alive. And they directly and deeply affect our concepts, our feelings, our relationships. They affect the way we look at life and God, at others and ourselves.

We preachers have often given people the mistaken idea that the new birth and being "filled with the Spirit" are going to automatically take care of these emotional hangups. But this just isn't true. A great crisis experience of Jesus Christ, as important and eternally valuable as this is, is not a shortcut to emotional health. It is not a quickie cure for personality problems.

Healing for Damaged Emotions, David Seamands, Victor Books, pages 11–12.

■ ■ ■

The ultimate goal is spiritual and emotional wholeness, and forgiveness is an important component of wholeness. You must acknowledge the hurt and the anger, but don't stay there. Move on to forgiveness. Take down the barriers. Face the hurt, the fear, and the anger. Understand what forgiveness really means and abandon your stubborn decision to hold on to the past.

In *The Hiding Place* Corrie ten Boom wrote about forgiving someone who had hurt her. Corrie and her sister, Betsie, had been imprisoned in concentration camps during World War II.

It was at a church service in Munich that I first saw him, the former S.S. man who had stood guard at the shower room door in the processing center at Ravensbruck. He was the first of our actual jailers that I had seen since that time. And suddenly it was all there—the roomful of mocking men, the heaps of clothing, Betsie's pain-blanched face.

He came up to me as the church was emptying, beaming and bowing. "How grateful I am for your message, Fraulein," he said. "To think that, as you say, He has washed my sins away!"

His hand was thrust out to shake mine. And I, who had preached so often to the people in Bloemendaal the need to forgive, kept my hand at my side.

Even as the angry, vengeful thoughts boiled through me, I saw the sin of them. Jesus Christ had died for this man; was I going to ask for more? Lord Jesus, I prayed, forgive me and help me to forgive him.

I tried to smile, I struggled to raise my hand. I could not. I felt nothing, not the slightest spark of warmth or charity. So again I breathed a silent prayer. Jesus, I cannot forgive him. Give me Your forgiveness.

As I took his hand the most incredible thing happened. From my shoulder along my arm and through my hand a current seemed to pass from me to him, while into my heart sprang a love for this stranger that almost overwhelmed me.

And so I discovered it is not on our forgiveness any more than on our goodness that the world's healing hinges, but on His. When He tells us to love our enemies, He gives, along with the command, the love itself.

Are you ready to forgive the people who have hurt you? The person you need to forgive may be deceased. The person may live far away. The person may not even know about the intensity of your feelings. Nevertheless, you need to forgive.

It may simply need to occur inside you. Or maybe you have done something to this person that necessitates not only dealing with this incident in your heart but also speaking a word to let him know that you have forgiven him.

Making Peace with Your Past, Tim Sledge, Lifeway Press, page 183.

■ ■ ■

As my husband's coffin entered the earth, a scrap of paper fluttered onto its lid—Luke's gift to a father he'd known so briefly. "I love you, Dad," he'd written in child-scrawl.

I embraced the silence, craved it. I wanted to be still for a long time, to heal and ponder this incomprehensible thing that had happened, to rant and shake my fist at God if need be. This was a pain so profound that the tears, the numbness, the disbelief, were all ripples on the surface of a deep, black pool of water. Nothing disturbed its depths. It seemed a well from which grief emanated, a core of my being I had reached only through extreme tribulation.

Yet I had children to raise who were as shaken and hurt as I, and a new baby coming. That lonely birth loomed ahead, a treacherous slope.

After two weeks, the kids were ready to return to school from sheer boredom. Relatives went home, and I resumed an unthinking housekeeping routine.

Little Luke proudly occupied his dad's empty place at the table as we sniffled through our first meal alone. "I can tell when you've been crying," said nine-year-old Naomi, running for the tissue box. "Your nose turns red." The box of tissues went round with the bowl of beans, and I'm not sure which was emptied first.

In a burst of energy, I tore the house apart that Easter, moving bed rails over the heads of startled guests, clearing a spot in my room for the baby. Might as well do the heavy work while men were around.

That was the nature of my grief, to hurry it up. Feel the pain and get it over with. I gave away Richard's clothes, clutching at the familiar smell and feel of that old sweater, his gray herringbone jacket.

I saved his wallet, still molded to the shape of his pocket. He could pull the most amazing things from that wallet—phone numbers and memorabilia from years gone by. I emptied his junk drawer, which, like every man's, held his special stones and pennies—the same treasures I'm sure he pocketed as a boy. Again I breathed his closeness, the small change of his life.

I took off my wedding ring very soon. It was uncomfortable to wear the symbol of a life that was no longer. Smooth from years of wear, its spot indented on my finger, the ring resisted being laid aside. My finger bore its mark for some time. I reached for it sometimes out of habit and was always startled to find it gone.

In some ways I had no choice but to hurry on. Self-pity and depression were indulgences my children would pay for. They tugged at me with the physical burden of their care, with worry over the emotional wounds they carried, with years of financial support to provide.

I didn't know the best way through such a tempest, but I found I could trust my instincts; I knew what was good for me. Like a physical wound that seeps and bleeds, the spirit also struggles to heal. I felt wounded, an amputee; even my appearance felt different. A wound heals slowly from the inside out; some never heal completely, and all grievous wounds leave scars.

One thing I knew with certainty: I had begun a grueling journey, one I might not survive without a massive infusion of grace. Without God, some part of me might die. This very clarity was a grace; I was poised on the brink of a mortal test, a great experiment. Were God's promises true and would they be enough?

I had no choice but to go forward in blind trust.

Young Widow, Kate Convissor, Zondervan, pages 22–23.

■ ■ ■

Have you counted the cost of the dream God has given you? Do you understand that God's call for you won't be without testing and trials and sometimes even sorrow? Understand that when you launch out to fulfill your dream you'll encounter challenges far above your own strength that can be fulfilled only in the strength of God.

Joseph was a dreamer, though he had no idea of the cost of his dream (see Gen. 37). He had a great future, yet it was with great consequence and great price. His brothers hated him and were full of jealousy and envy. Even his own father didn't understand his dream.

During Joseph's life he saw victories turn to defeat. He experienced disappointment with people. He was imprisoned without cause and lied about by those over him. It was thirteen long years before the God-given dream came to pass in his life.

The sufferings of Joseph, the dreamer, are recounted in Psalm 105:16-19. Verse 19 ends with this summary: "The word of the Lord tested him." Every dreamer will be tested and afflicted by those around him and even by God Himself. As the preacher observes in Ecclesiastes 5:3, "The dream comes through much effort."

Beyond Your Own Strength, Frank Damazio, Creation House, page 144.

CHAPTER TWO

KEEP TRACK OF GOD'S INVOLVEMENT IN THE EVERY DAY

God's dreams for us seldom unfold as quickly as we would like. That's frustrating, but the experience is not uncommon.

Do you remember the account in Scripture of young David being brought home from watching the flocks? Samuel was attempting to discover which one of Jesse's boys had been chosen by the Lord to replace Saul as king. Having looked over all the candidates presented to him, the prophet still had no positive word from the Lord. "Are these all the sons you have?" he asked.

"There is still the youngest," Jesse answered, "but he is tending the sheep." His comment implied that David was hardly of age to be a serious possibility. But when David got home, the Lord told Samuel, "Rise and anoint him; he is the one" (see 1 Sam. 16:1-13).

So God Himself said through His prophet that David was to be the next king. But many years would pass, involving any number of hair-raising escapades, before David would finally sit on Israel's throne. God's promise didn't come true immediately. In the meantime, I'm sure this former shepherd boy had frequent reason to doubt that the Lord's dream for him would ever be realized.

Here, then, is another barrier to seeing God's dreams validated in our lives. It's the inability to recognize His involvement in our everyday world and, therefore, giving up too soon on His long-range promises.

In the book *Tales of the Resistance* Scarboy doesn't become a hero overnight, either. But, like David, he truly is a hero. The question is whether or not he can hold on to what his King has promised, even if it isn't quickly realized. Scarboy's first battle in Enchanted City isn't with a giant like Goliath, but nevertheless his bravery is put to the test.

Din . . . din . . . din . . . The death drums were sounding another beat, faster and faster—a battle beat. Hero realized that more Burners and Breakers were gathering in striking formation. He had done a foolhardy thing. Even with the hatchet in hand, he was only one against many. He was in the middle of the Enchanter's territory, with no fellow Ranger to come to his aid. His only chance was in taking his opponents by surprise.

Rushing down the stairs, Hero swung into the battle tactic he had learned in the War of Fire in Great Park. "To the King! To the Restoration!" he cried, holding his hatchet with both hands. He jumped into the middle of the band of captured orphans. "Scatter!" he shouted. "Take off your blindfolds and run!"

With his weapon at arm's length, Hero began to whirl as the children scattered, climbing stairs, turning street corners, scurrying into holes. Round and round Hero whirled, cutting a circle of emptiness between himself and his would-be captors.

The Enchanter's men were so intent on taking him prisoner, they let the children escape. For a moment, Hero felt a defiant gladness.

S-C-A-R-B-O-Y! S-C-A-R-B-O-Y!

The Enchanter's evil eye had spotted him. The moment his old name was shouted, Hero began to freeze. His feet were leaden; the hatchet felt so heavy. Closer and closer inched the Burners and Breakers. One of the Breakers caught Hero's eye and held it with a stare; then he lifted his ugly cudgel over his head.

HARNK-HARNK! HARNK-HARNK! From opposite directions two taxicabs came careening down the narrow alley, their horns blaring, their speed frightening. *HARNK-HARNK!*

The Enchanter's men scattered, and the taxis screeched to a stop within inches of the stunned Hero.

"Need a ride, buddy?" A burly arm grabbed Hero and pulled him roughly into the front seat. As Hero frantically yanked the door shut behind him, his cab blasted into reverse and squealed around another corner. Within seconds a whole fleet of taxis raced out of alleys and side streets. They drove for a while in a straight line, and then veered off in opposite directions. *HARNK! HARNK! HARNK!* Their horns blared in great commotion, and for a moment Hero felt safe. No pursuer would know which cab had kidnapped him.

But was he under arrest or under protection?

Hero could just read the signs over the huge garage before the overhead door thudded shut behind them: City Taxi Company. There was a hustle as the driver detached from the power source. Hero's door was yanked open and he was pulled out.

"Ey, bub. Big Operator wants to see you in the terminal office." The cabbie jerked his head to the left, and then drove off. A man in uniform motioned Hero toward a glassed-in office.

The next thing he knew, his wrist was being clasped in the Ranger way. "Well, son. Most Rangers infiltrate Enchanted City as subtly as possible. The whole town knows you've arrived, not to mention the powers that be in the Dagoda. But welcome to the Resistance. We are all King's men and women here, working for the Restoration."

Hero's mouth dropped, and Big Operator smiled.

"Yessir, the dispatchers had themselves a job getting you out of that tight spot. It's not easy moving a taxi vanguard into position on a moment's notice.

"By the way, I think we picked up most of the orphans. That scattering tactic was pretty effective. The Resistance can use a man like you. How would you like to see the rest of the operation?"

The two walked to the middle of the taxi terminal, a large underground cavern with a huge map of Enchanted City on one wall. Big Operator pointed to purple paper flags stuck all over the map. "Sightings," he explained. "The King has been sighted all over the city. The Enchanter's nervous. . . . Our informants say the Dagoda's been a hot place with a whole lot of fire flying." . . .

Hero's mind would not stop whirling. He didn't know which question to ask first. "But—but what about the Enchanter? How do you get by with this in the middle of Enchanted City?"

Big Operator smiled, but it was a grim expression. He put his arm around the lad's shoulders. "Make no mistake. The Enchanter is evil and he's dangerous—never forget it. The closer the Restoration, the more Sightings of the King—the more dangerous and desperate he will become." Then his smile became almost cocky. "But the truth is, the Enchanter only has power over those who fear him. Here in the Taxi Resistance, we are subjects of the King. Consequently, we are not afraid."

Sightings of the King

There's something important here which, I believe, applies to all of life. When "sightings" of the King begin to multiply, our world starts to get exciting. How thrilling to hear that the Monarch's presence has been witnessed. God's bigger dreams quickly come into sharper focus when we're reminded of His involvement in our lives. When this happens, though, it's also true that the enemy engages us in fiercer combat.

Even so, I say, "Good for you!" to those who have trained themselves to recognize God in the every day. These are the men and women who find it easiest to sustain their belief in God's long-range dreams. That's because they see daily evidence that the Lord hasn't forsaken them.

It was that way with David. One "God sighting" occurred while, as a young refugee, he was hiding in a cave with his band of so-called outlaws. They were being tracked by King Saul and 3,000 chosen men. When the king had to relieve himself, lo and behold—he did so in the very cave where David was hiding. Then Saul decided to rest there awhile.

David's friends, far back in the cave, whispered that the Lord had given his enemy into his hands! "This isn't mere coincidence," they were saying in essence. "God's in it." But the only thing David did was to creep up unnoticed and cut off a corner of Saul's robe. David knew that in this incident God was saying, "I'm looking out for you, David. See how I can give Saul into your hands whenever I want!" (See 1 Sam. 24:1-4.)

There were numbers of situations like this in David's life. This specific event involved unusual linkage and timing. Of all the caves in that region, Saul chose the very one in which David and his men were hiding. It had to be more than chance that caused Saul to say, "Stop! That cave over there is going to be my restroom for the moment."

The point is, we all can maintain excitement about God's larger dreams for us when we keep close track of His involvement in our everyday world. Keeping close track of His involvement is important. I do it as part of my daily journaling. I've recorded thousands of such entries in my lifetime. What faith-builders they are.

This exercise is truly one of the most pleasurable aspects of my life. Seldom does a day go by when I don't see an obvious answer to prayer, some unexpected evidence of God's care, or maybe special help He provides to do His work in the world.

Possibly some of my "sightings" are coincidence, but I'm convinced an awful lot of them aren't. And one way or the other, I choose to give God the credit.

In the Bible we see that this is what David did too! He recorded what happened to him and acknowledged it as God's work. Psalm 57 is an example of such an account. It's a song of David praising the Lord for His help "when he had fled from Saul into the cave." Read these verses and picture yourself in David's situation.

Have mercy on me, O God, have mercy on me,
for in You my soul takes refuge.

I will take refuge in the shadow of Your wings
    until the disaster has passed.
I cry out to God Most High,
    to God, who fulfills His purpose for me.
He sends from heaven and saves me,
    rebuking those who hotly pursue me;
    God sends His love and His faithfulness.
I am in the midst of lions;
    I lie among ravenous beasts—
men whose teeth are spears and arrows,
    whose tongues are sharp swords.
Be exalted, O God, above the heavens;
    let Your glory be over all the earth.
They spread a net for my feet—
    I was bowed down in distress.
They dug a pit in my path—
    but they have fallen into it themselves.

My heart is steadfast, O God,
    my heart is steadfast;
    I will sing and make music.
Awake, my soul!
    Awake, harp and lyre!
    I will awaken the dawn.
I will praise You, O Lord, among the nations;
    I will sing of You among the peoples.
For great is Your love, reaching to the heavens;
    Your faithfulness reaches to the skies.
Be exalted, O God, above the heavens;
    let Your glory be over all the earth.

Hide-and-seek is a universal game. Everyone's played it at one time or another. In the Scriptures it's almost as if the Lord invites us to go on a spiritual hide-and-seek. "You will seek Me and find Me when you seek Me with all your heart." That's Jeremiah writing on God's behalf to the exiles in Babylon. " 'I will be found by you!' declares the Lord" (Jer. 29:13-14). So even when His people are captives in another land, it's as if the Lord tells them, "Don't stop looking for Me!"

The "fun factor" in looking for God comes out in a verse like Psalm 105:3, "Let the hearts of those who seek the Lord rejoice." And we do rejoice frequently when we see the Lord working in our lives.

"Seek and you will find." That's how Jesus issued the challenge in His Sermon on the Mount (Matt. 7:7). He was talking about the reality of His now-and-future kingship.

As I expressed earlier, one of the most pleasurable aspects of my own involvement in Christ's kingdom is writing down each day what I call my "God Hunt sightings." These are occasions when I see the Lord acting in my behalf in a special way, and I choose to attribute the events to Him. In our family we've come up with four categories that help define what we're talking about.

Answers to Prayer

One is an obvious answer to prayer. Let me illustrate. I hesitated attending a conference because I needed to prepare a rather complicated paper for a particular man. It was due the day I was to get back. I went to the conference anyway and was overjoyed to see that this person was also there. When I checked in at the hotel desk, I was so surprised I just said hello and walked on.

As soon as I got to my room I prayed, "Lord, I'm amazed this man is here. How wonderful it would be if we could talk for an hour or so and work through some of our concerns in person. But this is a huge conference. I may never run into him again. Please allow that to happen—I'll immediately ask him if there's a time we can meet while we're here."

I unpacked my things, went down on the elevator to the main lobby, and saw this man coming in the front door of the hotel again. We talked briefly and set a time to get together the next morning. To me that was a marvelous God Hunt sighting. The time together helped me immensely.

This might not seem like a God Hunt sighting to you, but, as I've already explained, I choose to give the Lord the credit for what happens on these occasions. I admit some of my "sightings" may be coincidence, but I prefer to believe most of them aren't! And what matters is not whether I can convince someone else, but whether I'm satisfied that it's the Lord at work.

Evidence of His Care

The second God Hunt category is unexpected evidence of His care.

I called from the office and asked my wife, Karen, "Where are you money-wise?" I needed to head home and pack. We were using some frequent flyer award tickets to take a couple of well-deserved days away. I had very little cash in the bank, although I figured we could use a credit card if need be. But maybe Karen had money.

Her answer was, "My bank account is as low as yours!"

"Just wondered," I responded. "See you soon."

In the next few moments an old friend stopped by the office and said, "Heard you and Karen were leaving for a few days. Knowing how you guys live, I thought you might need some cash. It's a gift; don't give it back. Have a good time. The Lord go with you."

Care of this sort is not an everyday occurrence. But I praise the Lord for friends and *also* for unexpected evidences like this of God's care.

Unusual Linkage or Timing

A third God Hunt category is unusual linkage or timing, such as when David hid in the very cave Saul decided to rest in. It was too perfect to be mere chance.

Unusual linkage and timing is getting on an almost empty airplane and sitting across the aisle from someone who desperately wants to know about Jesus and how to personally meet Him. God has provided an almost private setting and an hour and a half flight during which you are able to lead the person to the cross.

Help to Do His Work

A last God Hunt category is what we call help to do His work in the world. It's having a new family attend the church with the very skills needed to replace those of a strong couple who have just moved out of town. It's having a friend call and share a story that works perfectly for the closing illustration in a Sunday School lesson you've been working on. It's saying, as David did, "I need a friend, Lord — a friend who's like a brother. This future kingship assignment You've given me isn't an easy one." And the Lord responds, "David, I've prepared the king's son, Jonathan, to be that friend to you."

Those God Hunt categories, again, are:

1. An obvious answer to prayer
2. Unexpected evidence of His care
3. Any unusual linkage or timing
4. Help to do God's work in the world.

Occasionally a God Hunt sighting will fit several categories. That's no problem. And sometimes a sighting is almost in a category of its own. Don't worry about that either.

What's important is the belief that the Lord is constantly calling to us, "Seek Me. I'm here. I'm not that hard to find. Just look a little. Come on, now!"

Here's an important point. I believe it's necessary to write these sightings down. We need to keep a record of them. A list like this is great for reviewing when the dark days come. I make God Hunt sightings a regular part of my prayer journal.

To go on the God Hunt you may need to think in a new way. Some will have to learn to become like a child again, to renew that sense of wonder and delight. Others will need to break through a glass ceiling. Maybe you're not young like David was. That doesn't matter. It's never too late to start something good.

Beware when you no longer sense the joy of the daily God Hunt. What happens then is that we become secular, just like the world. To be secular means that we restrict the sacred life to an hour or two on Sunday morning, seldom seeing the supernatural interface with our everyday world. What a sad way to live . . . as secular Christians!

Let me return to *Tales of the Resistance.*

Big Operator gave the lad with the scar an unlikely assignment: Keeper of the Chronicle of Sightings of the

King. The chief of the Taxi Resistance knew that those who look harder for what they seek often find more than they expect.

"On-street sightings!" shouted Hero. "But—but I'm terrible at Sightings! I could hardly find the King in disguise in Great Park! How am I going to find him here in Enchanted City?" ... "But what about my scar? All of the Enchanter's men have a description of me by now. You yourself said there was a manhunt."

Big Operator was not moved. "I need an operator with street savvy and Ranger training. It's imperative that someone keep records of the King's activities. Hide your scar. Stay away from lights. The weather's turning cool; wear a scarf. Of course, this is a dangerous assignment. If you're afraid ..."

Hero started to say that it wasn't fear, but at that moment the buzzer in the terminal sounded the yellow alert, indicating that a taxi was approaching in haste. A mechanic began to crank up the great garage door. At the same moment, a dispatcher at the control panel shouted, "Sighting!" The King had made himself known somewhere in the city. With amazement, Hero and Big Operator watched two frightened children climb confusedly out of the back of the cab. The door slammed; an echo reverberated.

"Hey!" shouted the driver. "I left the King t'bring dese kids in—but the Enchanter's car's comin'! Better get back to action." The cabbie indicated the location of the Sighting to a monitor, "Heraldry post 101; Moire Oxan." A pin was immediately stuck in the map of Enchanted City.

"Wait a minute!" cried Big Operator, turning to the lad. "What do you say, Hero? I need a chronicler right now out on the street. Do you want to see the King in action? The taxi can take you back."

To see the King—at that moment Hero forgot all his doubts. He clasped Big Operator's wrist in the Ranger way, grabbed his bag, and hurried to hop into the front seat of the taxi.

Amanda turned from the control board, shoved back her headset and earphones, and called, "Where are you going?"

Hero slammed the taxi door shut. The cabbie gunned the motor as the mechanic began to crank up the great door again. Hero leaned out the window and grinned. "To the streets. I'm going to see the King!"

There's a lot more to this part of the tale than I've shared, but it ends this way ...

So Hero become the Keeper of the Chronicle of Sightings of the King. He was often in dangerous places, often filled with doubt; but he found more reason to believe than not to believe and he discovered for himself that in the Kingdom, where the King rules, believing is seeing.

That's what I want for you. I want you to learn that seeing—having to have everything proved so that no one could possibly doubt—isn't believing. But often believing is seeing as we learn to interpret what happens with eyes of faith, experience the joy of sighting the hand of God in our every day, become like children spiritually, accept God's invitation to play hide-and-seek, as we become skilled at God Hunt sightings, not missing a thing.

And because we keep track of His involvement in our daily lives, we're excited to believe God's longer-range dreams for us will come true as well!

FOR DISCUSSION AND REFLECTION

1. When is it that God seems most removed from your everyday world?

2. Who is a person you feel experiences the presence of the Lord in an unusual way? Why do you think this is so?

3. As you look back on your life, what is a God Hunt sighting you recall?

4. What do you like most about going on a daily God Hunt?

5. Is there anything about going on a daily God Hunt that seems intimidating? What?

6. Talk about a time you believe God put a long-range spiritual dream in your heart.

READINGS

While driving down a country road, a friend cried, "Oh, stop! There's bittersweet!" It was only when she pointed out the vines intertwined in the branches of the trees that I could see them. Then I wondered how I could missed the obvious touches of color in the late fall landscape.

My friend spotted the bright orange berries because she knew what she was looking for. She had trained her eye to see the beauty in the natural world, and she gathered the weeds and pods for lovely wreaths and arrangements. This visual keenness allowed her to see what other people could not.

We always find what we are looking for. When I was pregnant with each of our four children, it seemed as if the world was filled with other pregnant women! Our oldest son is an amateur ornithologist, and his eye spots birds on telephone wires or in soaring patterns that I never notice. David tells me how comfortable he is becoming with middle age; now that he is going grey, the world seems filled with other midlife, grey-haired men.

The same principle works when we are looking for God. Once the hunt truly begins, we see evidences of his Presence in all of life. We prayed, and a life was spared. There was no money, and an unexpected check came in the mail. We begin to see a pattern and think "God has walked in this place today."

Begin the God Hunt by looking back. Attempt to remember the times when you were convinced you had found evidence of God's presence. The supernatural encounter was startlingly real at the time. A miraculous healing took place in your extended family that people talk about to this day. You recall religious meetings where the room was filled with the power of the Holy Spirit.

Begin by thinking: *When I was a child, were there any times when I sensed that God was near to me?* Quickly jot down enough details to make the memory clear, and continue through the other stages of your life.

The God Hunt, David and Karen Mains, David C. Cook, pages 11–12.

■ ■ ■

Out of Billings the travel agent had me booked on a trunk airline flight north, and so I went to the desk to check in.

"Sorry, sir," the agent said, "but that flight's canceled for today."

"When's the next flight?" I asked.

"Not till seven tomorrow morning."

"But I've got to get there. I have a speaking engagement tonight."

"Sorry, sir."

I stepped away from the counter and silently thanked God for this disappointment, asking Him to show me the reason for it.

Just then another man stepped up to the counter, a big, burly character who, when he learned of the canceled flight, let out with an air-blueing stream of profanity.

"Look," he bellowed, "you get me on a flight! I'm gonna lose a lotta money if I don't get up there!"

"I'm sorry," the agent said meekly. "There's nothing I can do."

A third man came to check in for the flight. He too displayed his temper, though not so vociferously as the first.

I stepped up to the two men. "Since there are three of us," I said, "why don't we charter a plane?"

"Good idea!" the big fellow exclaimed. Turning to the agent he said, "Get us some information right away on charter flights!"

In a few minutes we were out beside a small plane. The big fellow sat up front with the pilot, we two smaller men in the back.

"My name is Malcom Randall," my companion introduced himself.

"I'm Stanley Tam," I said. "What's your business?"

"I work for the government. You?"

"I'm from Lima, Ohio. We reclaim and refine silver and also have a plastics sales organization."

"You're here on business?"

"I'm speaking at a church tonight, telling about my experiences as a Christian businessman."

"That's fascinating. I wish I could hear you, but I'll be tied up with appointments."

"Would you let me share some of my experiences with you now?"

"Sure, why not?"

So I began my story.

"Say," he interrupted, "I've heard you speak! It was at a service club or something."

His sudden outburst threw me off for a moment.

"Well, how about that?" I said.

"Yeah, I sure have." He pointed to a pin on his lapel. "It was at a Lion's Club meeting somewhere. I'm out of town a lot, but I always try to get to the local club wherever I happen to be. Isn't that something?"

It so intrigued him to have run across me before, I had difficulty getting back on course.

But finally he said, "Go ahead. Finish the story."

As I continued, he grew more intensely attentive. I could see evidence of spiritual concern creep across his countenance.

"You know," he said when I had concluded my testimony, "almost every night I get down on my knees and try to pray. I confess my sins."

"Do you have God's peace in your heart?" I asked.

He shook his head. "That's something I know nothing about," he said.

"May I tell you how to find this peace?" I asked.

He nodded.

Moments later there on the plane God honored me with the privilege of bringing another man to a personal knowledge of His Son.

"You know something," this man said to me, "it was no accident the plane was canceled out of Billings. It was an act of God. He knew I needed to meet you!"

God Owns My Business, Stanley Tam, Horizon House, pages 143–44.

■ ■ ■

"Oh, yuck!"

My daughter Laura stepped back and pinched her nose as I broke the neck of a hefty catfish, spilling its entrails into a blood-splattered bucket. Small price to pay for inch-thick, fresh fillets.

Small price, too, for building a relationship with the third fisher on this expedition, Jeremy.

Yesterday, sitting in my office for the first time, he wore a just-try-to-figure-me-out expression on his face. A high school senior, he came, he said, "just to keep peace with my mother." Two days before, Jeremy had been expelled for pulling a hunting knife on a classmate.

"So, why did you do it?" I asked.

Silence.

"What was going on in your thinker when you made your move?"

More silence.

"Look, I just want to be your friend," I said, but the words felt hollow.

"Prove it," his eyes said, then shifted to the wall on my right.

For more than an hour I tried to get through to him. But I felt like I was rowing around an island, getting a general view of things but not finding a place to land.

"I have a girlfriend at school," he said. They talk some, but not too much—afraid to get too close.

"Ever been hurt badly by someone?" I asked.

He admitted that he had, but he wouldn't talk about it with anyone, not even his mother. *Lord, help me,* I prayed. *This guy doesn't trust his own mother, much less a probing stranger.*

There, he did it again. Something on the wall to my right caught his eye. Oh, of course, the calendar. Nice picture: a swarthy Indian displaying his catch. Walleyed pike. I think.

I turned away, and then it hit me. I played my hunch.

"You like to fish?"

"Love it."

"Really?" *Thank you, Lord.* "Been fishing lately?"

"Naw, not since we moved to town. But when I was a kid, we lived next to the Tensaw River, and I used to go every chance I got. It's better to go when the water is high, where you can use a boat and set out a trout line overnight. Most of the time I caught catfish that way, and once I caught a fifteen pounder. But if the water is down, you wanna go for bream or bsss that hang out around the stumps—course, you hafta know what you're doing 'cause the water is hot and the fish are sluggish . . ."

On he went for ten minutes and wasn't even winding down when I interrupted, "It's been a while since I've hung a fish myself. I've got a good mind to fool some catfish in the morning. Would you go with me?"

"Are you serious?"

"Serious as a heart attack."

"I'll go. What time?"

"Let's make it seven-thirty, unless that's too early."

"Not for me. I'll buy the wrigglers."

The next day, we threw the little ones back and kept seven. The net scales tipped seventeen pounds. Jeremy was beaming.

"I'll clean 'em for you," he said.

He cleaned the first one, and I the next, tentatively curling my fingers around those dreadful spines.

"Sometime we should go hunting together," he offered.

Who would have guessed—all this prompted by a picture

on a wall calendar! And just two weeks earlier or later, that picture would not have been there.

I knew a Fisherman bigger than both of us was maneuvering the boat.

Arlin Schrock, "Fishing in Holy Water," *Leadership 7* (Summer 1991): 38–39.

■ ■ ■

Hundreds of thousands have been thrilled and challenged by the doctor's experiences in soul winning, such as he has recounted in *The Romance of a Doctor's Visits.* For example, in the account of "The Little Man in a Big City" he tells of his being alone in the great city of New York. Before he went out for a business appointment he had prayer in his hotel room, and requested: "My Lord, this is a large city of seven million people, and I am just a weak, unknown servant of Thine with no knowledge of the city and no acquaintance with the hungry hearts that may be there. Thou alone dost know whom Thou has been dealing with. Here is my body — my feet and my lips. Wilt Thou take them today to some troubled heart and speak through me Thy Words of light and life? Thank You, Lord, I believe You will do it."

As he walked eastward on Thirty-second Street he passed a stationery shop and noticed a small leather-covered notebook in the window. This brought to mind his need of a book in which to keep his prayer list. Upon entering the shop he inquired of the little German owner thereof about the notebook. The size and the price were satisfactory; and the shopkeeper began to wrap it up. Just then Dr. Wilson said. "Do you know what I expect to do with this little book?"

The storekeeper did not know, and was astonished to learn that it was to be used as a prayer book. Thereupon he began to unwrap the package saying, "I am sorry, my friend, but this is a blank book; it is not a prayer book."

That was just the opening Dr. Wilson needed. He explained that he made his own prayer book, using the left-hand pages for petitions and the right-hand ones for the answers. Then he added his testimony of knowing the Lord Jesus as His Saviour, and invited the shopkeeper to do the same.

The reply was not surprising. "Mister, I have tried to find Gott for many years. I have gone around Manhattan and Brooklyn and the Bronx, night after night, attending many services, but failed always to find Gott. Can you tell me how to get Him?"

After explanation of the Scripture that the Lord Jesus is the Way, the Truth, and the Life, Dr. Wilson led his new friend to the Saviour. The quest of the years had come to an end, for now the shopkeeper knew the Lord Jesus for himself.

And for the soul-winner only twenty minutes had elapsed from the prayer in the hotel room to the winning of another soul to Christ, because the life and lips of the servant belonged to the Holy Spirit.

They Found the Secret, V. Raymond Edman, Zondervan, pages 127-28.

■ ■ ■

On the Saturday before the crucial congregational meetings, John Maxwell and his 100 prayer partners went out to what they believed would be the future site of Skyline Wesleyan. The more they prayed, the more they began getting a strange feeling, first individually, then in groups. After unimaginable agonizing, they began to admit to each other that collectively they were hearing God say, "This is not your site!"

At the congregational meeting the next evening, John rehearsed the process they had gone through to decide to purchase the property. It had seemed right from the business point of view, from the financial point of view, from the church management point of view, and from advice they had received from many sources. But one thing could outweigh all those positive indications—the word from the Lord received through earnest and effective prayer.

Even though Maxwell knew that many would be disappointed, he had built up enough faith in the hand of God working in his life and the life of the church through his prayer partners that he became bold. He recommended that Skyline Wesleyan Church withdraw the offer for the property. He also assured the congregation that if God was really telling them not to buy this property, it was because He had something much better in store for them. How much better no one could have imagined at the time!

The search process began once again. They located a beautiful 80-acre property and asked the owners twice if they would sell, but they were turned down both times. The prayer partners and others continued to pray. Soon a financial crunch came and the owners seemed more disposed to sell. Skyline made a very low bid of $1.8 million for the 80 acres, and the owners by then were in such a tight situation they reluctantly said they would sell. But the owners insisted on some fine print: If Skyline could not get the land zoned for a church, they would agree not to sell the land but would return the land and also pay the owners interest on the amount Skyline had spent.

The church, cognizant of the risk, closed the deal only to find out through an independent appraiser that the true value of the land was $4.5 million. Skyline Church had taken an even greater risk than they thought!

The church was also forced to buy three times the number of shares of water rights than necessary, and they paid $120,000 for them. But drought set in on Southern California, the value of the water rights soared, and the owners begged them to sell two-thirds of the rights back. By that time the two-thirds were worth $250,000 and as part of the deal, the church persuaded the former owners to rescind the clause that they would have to give back the property if it were not zoned for their use. So God gave them the property for the price they had offered with no fine print, along with an extra $130,000!

But that is not all. They had the "80-acres" surveyed and found that the land was really 110 acres! Then the Water District needed 10 acres on the low part of the land and offered to trade 30 acres at the top, right where John Maxwell had envisioned the parking lot, for the 10. They now had 130 acres. Finally they were offered $4 million for a stretch of industrially-zoned land, which they did not need for the church anyway.

Skyline Wesleyan now has a lovely church site, probably worth more than $10 million, for which they ended up not paying a thing!

This was all because of prayer. Through prayer, the pastor's prayer partners had heard God say, No. Their spiritual maturity caused them to be bold enough to follow what they knew would be an unpopular course of action. Once they followed, they began hearing a series of yesses from God that carried them, their pastors, the church board, and the congregation over the threshold and into the greatest era of Skyline Wesleyan's history.

Prayer Shield, C. Peter Wagner, Regal, pages 21–23.

CHAPTER THREE

BREAK OUT OF OUR COMFORT ZONES

When I wake up I seldom remember what I've dreamed. People amaze me when they can recall not only what they've dreamed about, but the details as well.

In a similar fashion, when dreaming God's dreams, I sometimes find it hard to get them into sharp focus. That's because He doesn't always show me precisely what He has in mind. His dreams remain a bit fuzzy. Maybe that's the nature of dreams.

The Old Testament character Abraham knew what it was like to follow a divine dream without knowing all the details. God had promised that he would be the father of many nations, but as the years progressed, he passed the normal fathering age. Yet Abraham continued to believe the Dream Giver because he considered Him to be faithful. Later in Genesis we see the picture of this old man and his miracle son walking up Mt. Moriah to sacrifice to God. Once again, Abraham must have questioned how God's dream could be fulfilled if he sacrificed Isaac.

Another picture comes to mind from the New Testament, where people who heard God's call must have wondered what He was really asking of them. Recall the fishermen (Simon, Andrew, James, and John) leaving their nets because Jesus called to them, "Follow Me . . . and I will make you fishers of men" (Matt. 4:19). But what did that challenge mean? It would take a lifetime for them to find out. Even so, what a privilege to begin dreaming God's dreams for them. That sure offered more sizzle than a lifetime spent in the fresh fish business.

Would you be excited if God said to you, "I have a dream I want you to share in"?

I'm sure that sounds good! And I don't want to discourage you. But this chapter underscores that those who accept God's invitation to dream His dreams usually have to break out of what I would call their "comfort zones." Such an invitation is extended to Thespia, a young actress in the book *Tales of the Resistance*. She is "the most beautiful player of all."

The Dagoda of the Enchanter loomed in the middle of Enchanted City, so that none would forget the watching eye of the fire wizard. Close by, and a happier place was the Palace of Players. Here the people of the city, filled with weariness and heartsickness, came and forgot for a time their griefs and fears and pains.

Thespia stood in the wings of the stage brushing her long and luxuriant hair. She was the most beautiful of all the players and even now she could hear the house chanting her name. "Thespia! We want Thespia!" Many suiters sought her hand, but she turned them all away.

"Flowers from the Dagoda!" the assistant stage manager called. Thespia yawned and instructed that the gift be delivered to her suite in the Palace.

"Four minutes! Four minutes!" the callboy warned. Thespia straightened her gown and took one last look in the mirror.

Through a crack in the thick velvet curtain, she could see that the theater was full. It was almost time for the play to begin. *Poor ones. Poor, poor ones. Forget for a while, then home again only to remember your empty half-lives.* She whispered this hollow blessing over them.

"See you t'night," the lead actor shouted as he hurried to take his position. "QUIET!" warned the stage director.

"But . . ." Thespia wanted to protest to the actor;
then she shrugged her shoulders and turned to wait for
that always-thrill, the curtains rising and the stage filling
with the sudden radiance of spotlights, then the sono-
rous voices of trained players. She particularly loved
tonight's play. *The Return of the King* had been banned
for years, but recently several very old myth cycles had
been restored to the Palace repertoire.

We need a king—Thespia quickly looked around as
though the stagehands could read her innermost mind.
Treason, this thinking; she knew it. Careful, or the most
beautiful player of all could play a final role tied to a
stake at Burning Place. The first rule all children of
Enchanted City learned after branding was:

THERE IS NO SUCH THING AS A KING.
DEATH TO PRETENDERS!

Senseless! she thought, and looked around again. If
there's no such thing as a king, why such a fuss? The
placards, the lectures, the propaganda songs—". . . no
king, no king, the Enchanter's the thi-ng." Silence
would have helped her to forget, but each protest made
her wish all the more: *If only there really were a king!*

I believe everyone dreams that dream. If only there really
were a king, a good and righteous king.

Certainly the destitute of the world hold to such a dream.
But then, I believe, so do the most beautiful of entertainers,
the most influential of leaders, even the most monied and
educated and acclaimed.

We are the ones who know there really is a King, aren't
we?

Once His dream for this world had first place in our hearts.
Now maybe the dream seems a bit fuzzy. It's not as clear as
it was before. Possibly other dreams have crowded it out.
We're not as willing to take the risks we once took to see
that dream fulfilled. We're older now, more guarded.

"Three minutes! Three minutes!"

As a lonely understudy, Thespia had determined to be the finest player in all Enchanted City. Unlike the other actresses, who became arrogant and haughtily cut all ties with their pasts, Thespia perfected her art in the streets. She refused to become enamored with the sterile practice rooms, the posh living suites, and the luxuries of the Palace of Players. She bound up her flaxen hair with common cloth and walked the marketplace, listening to how real people spoke words.

Often she went back to her own people, to Moire Oxan where they lived, to the stacked hovels where she had been raised. There she carried old grannys' burdens that weighed their bent backs double and she brought tidbits of food for the always-hungry waifs. She wept when orphans were taken away to the Orphan Keeper and she felt the cold whistling through these always night lives, and remembered what it was to never have enough fire or power.

Their pain became her own, and their small and meagre joys as well. Because she did not despise them, she was loved: and it was they, the street people sitting on the gallery floor, who called her name.

One night, one terrible night, her cousin's wee babe wriggled in agony in Thespia's arms while searchers hunted its mother who was foraging in a city-edge workshift. It squinched up its tiny face, took a last, long breath, and died. Shuddering with sobs, Thespia hid in a tower of the Players' Palace. How could she act the next night, play the comic, with this terrible knowledge—that babies died who shouldn't die in Enchanted City. She grieved with new understanding—there was little she, or anyone, could do.

Another woman we know of had similar feelings once about there being little she could do. She was a real-life orphan living in the citadel of Susa in Persia. This young woman had been raised by an older cousin, Mordecai. The Scriptures state that she was "lovely in form and features"

(Es. 2:7). In fact, she was designated the most beautiful of all the virgins in the vast domain of King Xerxes, and she was made queen.

Her role was to be a good wife to the king. Apparently that was the unique reason the Lord had brought her into the world. It wasn't an easy job because her husband had a bad temper. But then it wasn't the worst of assignments, either.

Breaking Out of Your Comfort Zone

Be careful, however, Esther. Don't get too used to the good life. The Lord may someday ask you to break out of your comfort zone and participate in His larger dream. Soon too! So don't wrap your fingers too tightly around what you've been given. Hold on to things lightly, with an open palm if possible—the court, the clothes, the queen's crown.

Those things might have represented Esther's comfort zone.

What's yours?

The position?
The salary?
The business you own?
The house?
The family?
The friendships?
The approval of parents?
The good life you live?
Your attractive appearance?
Your retirement package?
Your investments?
The recognition?
The title?

What symbol represents for you what the court and clothes and crown symbolized for Esther—or what the stagelights, the costumes, the applause, the leading roles symbolized for Thespia?

Do you know?

Let me warn you not to hold on to such items too tightly.

Don't clamp your fingers around them. Instead, hold those things with an open hand.

You see, the real King might soon be saying, "I have a dream I want you to share in. Does that sound good to you? Do you think that if necessary, you could break out of your comfort zone? Could you put all you have at My disposal?"

Twenty million dollars—that's a lot of money. Well, it wasn't really $20 million as such, it was 10,000 talents of silver. But 10,000 talents of silver in the citadel of Susa would have been worth about 20 million dollars today. That isn't what the Lord was asking of Esther. He wanted her to put her very life on the line.

An evil man, Haman, had offered out of his fortune to place 10,000 talents into the royal treasury. The sum was enormous because the request that accompanied it was also. What Haman wanted was the privilege of killing all the Jews in the 127 provinces ruled over by King Xerxes. This monarch took the signet ring from his finger—his symbol—and gave it to Haman with the fateful words, "Do with the people as you please" (Es. 3:11).

It was then that cousin Mordecai made contact with the grown orphan girl he had raised. Esther had become queen of the land without revealing that she was Jewish. Mordecai encouraged her to beg her husband, the king, for mercy for her people. Mordecai wanted her to risk all she had been given—the comforts of the court, the title, the crown. This is the message he sent Esther.

Do not think that because you are in the king's house you alone of all the Jews will escape. For if you remain silent at this time, relief and deliverance for the Jews will arise from another place [God will do His "thing" no matter what], but you and your father's family will perish. And who knows but that you have come to royal position for such a time as this? (Es. 4:13-14)

Esther had no problem seeing God's hand in all that was happening. *This is why I've been given what I have,* she reasoned, *my beauty, my marriage, my throne.* She replied to

Mordecai, "Go, gather together all the Jews who are in Susa, and fast for me. Do not eat or drink for three days, night or day. I and my maids will fast as you do. When this is done, I will go to the king, even though it is against the law. And if I perish, I perish" (Es. 4:16).

So often we learn from Scripture that to be a part of God's dreams for us we must become spiritual risk-takers. We have to break out of our comfort zones. We need to dare to dream.

In chapter 1, I introduced this prayer:

Lord,
Daring to dream again sounds so good,
But sometimes memories of broken dreams haunt me.
Help me let go of the pain
That keeps me from responding to Your gentle nudgings.
Your presence encourages me to set aside fear
And to become a spiritual risk-taker.
I want Your dreams for me to be my dreams as well.
AMEN

Don't overlook the value of this prayer. When prayed repeatedly, it will keep before you the desire to risk all to see God's dreams for your life come true.

I'd also suggest once again that you figure out what represents your comfort zone. Get an actual picture of it that you can put in your Bible. The bank account, the new home, the family, the position. For me it's my calendar, my daily planner. That may not make much sense to you, but with all my deadlines I find that my life is almost slave to a schedule. If the Holy Spirit has a message for me, it's almost as if my response is, "I can talk Thursday at 2:00, Lord. How's that?"

So my comfort zone picture is a sheet from my calendar. This is the entrapment from which I have to break free. I put the calendar sheet in my Bible so that the Scriptures can stretch me. Have you noticed they do this if we let them, if our comfort zones don't crowd out what the Lord wants to say to us through His Word?

Well, Thespia, the most beautiful player of all, was open to the young King's moving her out of her comfort zone. Let's return to that story. The play *The Return of the King,* has begun.

"P-s-s-s-t, Thespia," the prompter hissed. "Entrance!"

She stepped onto the stage, her hair tumbling in captured stagelight, glowing like a halo. There was a gasp from the gallery and applause from the boxes. She closed her eyes and evoked the memory of the roseate sun, rising, rising—and stood shimmering beneath the overhead spotlights. "Oh, we are mortals and have forgotten how to laugh. Who will show us where laughter is hiding?" Thespia's lashes glistened with tears because it was true, so true.

Perhaps Thespia's power came from the gallery, from the men and women and children sitting on the floor and wearing ragged, tattered clothes. They, too, wondered where the laughter had gone. Most players acted to the boxes, to the rich patrons dripping with furs, sitting in plush chairs, their stomachs full. But Thespia played to the floor, to the people. She looked at them with pity. Eager, the whole mob lifted their heads to the stagelight, their mouths open, their eyes wide with wonder.

Thespia loved to make them laugh, loved their unsophisticated whooping, howling, and floor pounding. She loved to make them weep, to spill the overflow of sorrow that became dammed in the dark horrors of Enchanted City.

Tonight beyond the circle of reflected stagelight, she thought she saw a man standing, but he was in the gallery shadow. *Strange. Why don't the ushers have him sit or leave?*

Two stage beats, a pause. At this moment, the actor/king stepped from the wing. This was one of the play's dramatic moments, the actual return of the King; but suddenly, the lights flickered and dimmed. A groan went up from the theater.

"Power out! Oh-h-h-h-h-h. Power out!"

Even the players on stage moaned.

"Lights! Lights! Lights!" shouted the street people.

"Doesn't anything ever work in this wretched city!" In dismay Thespia realized she had spoken out loud. The actor/king leaned close to her, *"Careful!* Rumors say there's revolt underfoot."

But then Thespia realized that a light *was* shining in the darkened auditorium. The man she had seen in the gallery shadow seemed to be standing in his own light. She gasped and took a closer look; he seemed vaguely familiar. From the back of the hall, he raised his hand in greeting. Shyly, hardly realizing she did so, she reached out her hand toward him.

And the theater quieted as all watched the man walk within a center of radiance to the orchestra pit. He perched upon the rim, apologized to the musicians, and vaulted up to the stage. "This is where I make my entrance, I believe," he said, and his voice was wonderful, filled with the echo of faraway hills and laughing country streams.

He stood in the middle of the stage and held out strong arms. "There is a real kingdom," he announced, "and a real king."

Without knowing that they moved, all the players took one step closer to his warmth. Some in the gallery rose to their knees.

The man motioned to the conductor. "Music," he said, and the orchestra began to play. "Up tempo." The beat quickened in the percussion section and wound its way in and out among the street people whose feet began to tap.

"In the Kingdom of Light, there is no night."

And the man smiled at the gallery, at all in the house and at the players onstage. The beat waltzed its way to the tiers of boxes, and even a few of the wealthy patrons began to clap: *Ta-dum-ta-dum-ta-da-da-dum.*

"In the Kingdom of Light," the man chanted, "the day shines bright."

The music was infectious. Now many chanted back, "In the Kingdom of Light, the day shines bright."

Ta-da-ta-da-ta-da-da-dum, played the orchestra. The man raised his hands for quieter music.

"Have you ever heard of a kingdom where outcasts were welcomed?" the man asked.

And the people answered, "No-o-o-o-o!"

"Have you ever heard of a kingdom where every orphan had a home?"

"No-o-o-o-o-o-o-o!"

"Or where those who loved light could live in it? Or where those who sought for a king found him?"

The man lowered his voice to a stage whisper, and the whole audience leaned forward to hear, "In the Kingdom of Light, everything's right!"

Ah-h-h-h-h-h-h-h, sighed the house. And for a moment, everyone in the audience knew this was no play, no myth cycle dragged out of the palace archives. *"Ah-h-h-h-h-h-h,"* sighed the gallery again, a long sigh. If only there were such a place, such a real place.

The man offered his arm to the actor-king standing on one side of him and his other arm to Thespia who also stood near. She looked out on the audience and gasped—the people in the gallery were clothed in warm garments, their runny sores were healed, they were clean and healthy. This couldn't be true. She blinked her eyes and stared again and realized she was seeing the people through the glow of the man's light.

Tears ran down her cheeks, real tears, not player's tears. If it could only be; if there really were such a place. "Wh-wh-who are you?" she asked, and he answered, "You know who I am." Sobs broke her words, "But h-how do w-we find this kingdom of w-which you speak?"

He turned, took both her hands in one hand, and wiped away her tears. The other players gathered close, and one put his arm around Thespia's shoulders to comfort her.

"Follow me," said the man. "The real kingdom is wherever I walk and whenever anyone walks with me."

Thespia knew. He was wearing common clothes, the

plain garments of the people, but she wanted to fall at his feet and bow. Tears blurring her vision, she turned from the man, faced the audience, and walked to the edge of the stage. She stretched one hand to him and one hand to the gallery, as if in introduction. "The King," she said. "My Lord, the people."

Suddenly, the lights blinked off-on; the man-made power was coming up. Someone in the boxes shouted: THERE IS NO SUCH THING AS A KING! DEATH TO PRETENDERS! And several began to chant: DEATH! DEATH!

The orchestra stopped playing and all the notes tumbled together and fell in a heap, and the man-made power suddenly came fully on and the lights blazed forth. The audience shifted in their seats and patted their clothes straight. What a strange play—it must be intermission—but then all these old myth cycles were odd. They stood to stretch. And the magical moment was gone and the players exited, trying to remember what lines had been said and which lines remained to be said and who had the last cue; and the stage director didn't know which act to call next.

I have prayed even as I've been putting this chapter together that this might be a magical spiritual moment for you. It's never too late to dream.

"Follow Me," said Jesus to the fishermen in the Gospels, and they left their nets. Their response was like that of Abraham in the Old Testament. He stepped out in faith because God said, "I have a new place I want you to move. Can you leave the comfort of where you are?"

Let me rephrase Mordecai's challenge from the Book of Esther. The Lord will do His thing. If not through you, through someone else. But don't miss this opportunity— don't opt for the comfort zone.

* Be more vocal in your witness.
* Say, "Lord, as Your steward, I acknowledge that the money, the savings—they're really Yours."

* Pray, "God, if You have a new assignment for me, I'm ready."
* Be willing to break a glass ceiling if doing so makes for entry into a new world.

The Scriptures can come alive for you again! Realize that to dream God's dreams, all of us must become spiritual risk-takers. Overcome any barriers that hold you back, including inappropriate comfort zones. Let your response to the King be like that of Thespia.

Thespia stayed beside the man, who was buttoning his coat as though he meant to go. "Are you leaving?" she asked.

"Yes, the moment for believing is gone."

She held her breath. "C-can I come with you?"

He bowed and took her hand and kissed it; then he helped her climb as gracefully as possible over the orchestra pit, and they walked down the aisle and left the theatre together. And very few seemed to see them go.

And Thespia became a street player in the back alleys and dead ends of Enchanted City, acting out the King's story in such a way that all who saw her suspected— then hoped—that there was a real kingdom. Like the King, she worked in common clothes, and she never gave the luxuries of the Palace a backward glance, because when one has found one's real love it is easy to leave what has only been pretend.

FOR DISCUSSION AND REFLECTION

1. What are some unhealthy comfort zones Christians sometimes settle into?

2. Tell about someone you know who risked breaking out of comfortable confines.

3. When in the past have you been a spiritual risk-taker?

4. What are ways you presently see yourself responding to God's gentle nudgings?

5. The Daring to Dream Again Prayer reads, "Your presence encourages me to set aside fear. . . ." How is fear a factor in your spiritual walk?

6. What safeguards are there to keep spiritual risk-taking from getting out of hand?

READINGS

But I do not so easily return to the fray when I've been intimidated. I do not automatically walk back into the fire when I've been burned. My instinct is to go where the environment is cordial, warm, and affirming. Left to my feelings, I will avoid the conflict—stay out of the community when I've been threatened, choose another class when I've been attacked by the professor. My natural response is to protect my emotional comfort.

But God calls me not to emotional comfort but to obedience. I am to drive back through the woods where drunken men point guns in my face, not out of feeling but out of conviction, not because of the heart but because of the head. Risk is never a matter of the heart; it's always a matter of the will. I do not risk because I feel like it. I risk because of what God wants me to do.

But my head does not so easily take control. I am a rational creature, yes, but I am also created with glands and hormones, palms that sweat in fear and muscles that tighten in anger. What do I do with the emotional side of my nature? How do I rise above it and free myself for risk?

If I would know risk, I must confront the two sides of myself that fight for dominance. My feelings tell me to stay away from Blairston and his oral interpretation course. My reason says to complete the quarter. There are only six more weeks. I must decide whether reason or feelings will rule. If I follow feelings, where will they lead me? I will get an incomplete and will have wasted the entire quarter. Where will following my reason lead? To restoration with Dr. Blairston, at least on my part. To a grade. To the satisfied feeling that I did not run from a tough situation.

If I would learn to risk emotional discomfort, sometimes, away from the heat of the moment, I may need to stop and take a more general inventory. Do feelings or reason dictate the majority of my responses? Are my feelings keeping me from doing things I need to do, things I believe God would have me do? Is hospitable environment more important than obedience? Comfort more important than conviction?

If I would know risk, conviction must always be my criterion. I must obey whether I feel like it or not. I must drive through the woods even when I am scared. I must face Dr. Blairston even when I've been humiliated by him.

If I would know risk, I must be willing to walk without receiving positive emotional strokes from those around me. I must be willing to be unpopular with certain people, unwelcome in certain places. With Jesus, I must follow the dusty roads of Galilee toward Jerusalem, even though I know the cross awaits me there—the ultimate unwelcome.

Beyond Safe Places, Ruth Senter, Harold Shaw, pages 94–96.

■ ■ ■

Let him assume that the first ardours of his conversion might have been expected to last, and ought to have lasted, forever, and that his present dryness is an equally permanent condition. Having once got this misconception well fixed in his head, you may then proceed in various ways. It all depends on whether your man is of the desponding type who can be tempted to despair, or of the wishful-thinking type who can be assured that all is well. The former type is getting rare among the humans. If your patient should happen to belong to it, everything is easy. You have only got to keep him out of the way of experienced Christians (an easy task now-a-days), to direct his attention to the appropriate passages in Scripture, and then to set him to work on the desperate design of recovering his old feelings by sheer will-power, and the game is ours. If he is of the more hopeful type, your job is to make him acquiesce in the present low temperature of his spirit and gradually become content with it, persuading himself that it is not so low after all. In a week or two you will be making him doubt whether the first days of his Christianity were not, perhaps, a little excessive. Talk to him about "moderation in all things." If you can once get him to the point of thinking that "religion is all very well up to a point," you can feel quite happy about his soul. A moderated religion is as good for us as no religion at all—and more amusing.

The Screwtape Letters, C.S. Lewis, Lord and King Associates, pages 54–55.

■ ■ ■

Only 4 out of 10 pastors claim their church is completely or mostly open to new styles of ministry. A number of pastors expressed disappointment that their people are unwilling to experiment with new formats for ministry or are unwilling to take risks in the development of new programs, strategies and activities.

"Creatively, I feel stifled," bemoaned one minister. "People always resist change, but it seems that within the church we major on trying to retain what we've always done just so we won't have to take a chance. I'm quite concerned that this mentality is spreading and can only impair our ability as individuals and as a community to grow."

The resistance to new styles was most keenly felt by pastors of small churches. Whereas 6 out of 10 pastors of larger churches felt the freedom to try new things, only 1 out of 3 pastors in churches of fewer than 50 people felt the same sense of liberty.

Today's Pastors, George Barna, Regal, page 88.

■ ■ ■

I beheld, then, that they all went on till they came to the foot of the hill Difficulty, at the bottom of which was a spring. There were also in the same place two other ways besides that which came straight from the gate: one turned to the left hand, and the other to the right, at the bottom of the hill; but the narrow way lay right up the hill, and the name of the going up the side of the hill is called Difficulty. Christian now went to the spring, and drank thereof to refresh himself (*Isa. xlix. 10-12*); and then he began to go up the hill, saying —

'The hill, though high, I covet to ascend;
The difficulty will not me offend;
For I perceive the way to life lies here.

Come, pluck up heart, let's neither faint nor fear;
Better, though difficult, the right way to go,
Than wrong, though easy, where the end is woe.'

The other two also came to the foot of the hill; but when they saw that the hill was steep and high, and that there were two other ways to go—and supposing also that these two ways might meet again with that up which Christian went, on the other side of the hill—therefore they resolved to go in those ways. Now the name of one of those ways was Danger, and the name of the other Destruction. So the one took the way which is called Danger, which led him into a great wood; and the other took directly up the way to Destruction, which led him into a wide field, full of dark mountains, where he stumbled and fell, and rose no more.

I looked then after Christian, to see him go up the hill, where I perceived he fell from running to going, and from going to clambering upon his hands and his knees, because of the steepness of the place. Now, about the midway to the top of the hill was a pleasant arbour, made by the Lord of the hill for the refreshment of weary travellers. Thither, therefore, Christian got, where also he sat down to rest him. Then he pulled his roll out of his bosom, and read therein to his comfort; he also now began afresh to take a review of the coat or garment that was given to him as he stood by the Cross.

Thus pleasing himself awhile, he at last fell into a slumber, and thence into a fast sleep, which detained him in that place until it was almost night; and in his sleep his roll fell out of his hand. Now, as he was sleeping, there came one to him, and awakened him, saying, 'Go to the ant, thou sluggard; consider her ways, and be wise.' (*Prov. vi. 6.*) And with that Christian suddenly started up, and sped him on his way, and went apace till he came to the top of the hill.

The Pilgrim's Progress, John Bunyan, Collins, pages 56–57.

■ ■ ■

Letting go of possessions breaks the bonds of comfort. But if I want to be freed all the way, in the biblical sense, if I want to go beyond giving up what isn't needed, the next step is for me to prayerfully listen to my conscience, then to take risks. Not just any risks, but the risks that God demands.

Sometimes we are too safe to be alive. Stripping oneself of wealth takes away the numbness only for a while, if the soul is not transformed. For wealth itself is not the problem. It's my attitude—an attitude of fear that makes me protect myself excessively, that demands comfort. It's that attitude that determines whether or not I stay trapped inside the cocoon, trapped in soft and sleepy blindness. And when that protective attitude stands in the way, there's nothing that can substitute for simply *doing the difficult thing*.

It may be as small as stopping to help a stranger stranded on the highway. It may be driving into the city one night a week and parking in a rough neighborhood so I can serve at a soup kitchen. It may be even larger—taking in a rent-free boarder who needs a safe home, changing my job, adopting a child. These risks, made with such effort, will wrench me back into reality. They are like fresh air introduced into a garage full of carbon monoxide.

Without listening to God, I do not know what is truly healthy for myself. Risking for risk's sake is not the answer. But risking for God's sake is. And God is always wanting us to risk for his sake, just as his Son Jesus did. Thankfully, he knows that taking such risks is difficult, and he will not ask more than we can give.

On a flight out of Ethiopia several years ago, I met a gentle, kind-spirited man who took unusual interest in my wife and me. He seemed delighted to meet us and he was curious to know our stories, as well as to share his own. He turned out to be chairman for the board of a major relief-and-development organization.

Hamilton was there with a film crew, making a documentary on hunger in East Africa. In fact, as I learned from a crew member, he had paid for most of the filming out of his own pocket. During our conversation, he admitted reluctantly that he was an attorney by trade. For years he had made his living (and apparently a very good one at that) by doing legal work, but he had never found satisfaction in it. Then he became involved with relief-and-development work.

"For the first time, I felt as if my life had meaning," he said, laughing sheepishly. "I mean that. As an attorney, you've got to wonder sometimes if you have any meaning at all."

In my opinion, Hamilton showed that he had broken out of the shell of comfort. No person enslaved to security would have risked going into Ethiopia at that time—when Eritrean rebels had pushed within eighty miles of Addis Ababa and when Colonel Mengistu was rumored to be on the verge of toppling from power. Nor would he have traveled into the destitute areas where this film crew had to work, risking the diseases that rage through. But Hamilton had, and as a result he was spiritually alive. He had been set free from the illusion that his comfort, like Aling Nena's Virgin Mary, would somehow magically make life livable, worthwhile. To him, it was a delight that people around the world were coming to Christ because they saw Christians like himself giving of their wealth and risking involvement, no matter how stressful or dangerous that might be.

Hamilton was unusual. He had the strength to become spiritually alive while staying wealthy. Most do not have that strength. Saint Francis, for one, knew that he needed to break from wealth altogether. He literally stripped the clothes off his body so that they would not stand between him and God. He did not want any comfort if it meant captivity.

But Francis was rewarded for his action with riches beyond compare, for in taking that step he learned the truth stated so well by Thomas à Kempis, a monk who lived only one hundred years later, in the fourteenth century: "O my soul, thou can'st not be fully comforted, nor have perfect refreshment, except in God, the Comforter of the poor, and Patron of the humble."

Each of us needs to be set free from comfort. We need to ask, *How much do I really need?* Any more can become a trap. And to prove our willingness to live with less, we need to take the risks that God asks of us. There is wonderful liberation in letting go.

The Comfort Trap, Tim Bascom, InterVarsity, pages 58–60.

CHAPTER FOUR

BECOME WORLD-CLASS CHRISTIANS

People don't like it when somebody does them dirty. Most write their enemies off. They usually aren't open to extending any form of friendship to them. If given the opportunity to return the ill favor, they relish doing what they can to make life harder for those who've hurt them. The thought that someday maybe they could be good friends is the last thing they would dream of.

But that's not how the Lord is! His dreams for all who have offended Him is that someday they would be wooed back into a loving relationship. God's dreams are incredible in that regard.

Jonah was a prophet who found out the hard way what God's heart is like. The last thing in the world he wanted to do was to hold a preaching crusade in Nineveh, capital of Assyria. Talk about a rotten assignment!

Think about it: Would you as a North American want to preach Christ in an open-air crusade next week in Baghdad? How do you suppose Saddam Hussein would feel about it? That's the kind of challenge God gave Jonah. Assyria was the most feared nation of his day — the reigning superpower. And, unlike modern-day Iraq, Assyria hadn't been defeated in a recent war.

In the second verse of the small Old Testament book that bears this prophet's name, God says, "Go to the great city of

Nineveh and preach against it, because its wickedness has come up before Me."

It most certainly was a great capital city. Its size was huge for that time: 600,000 inhabitants, all living comfortably behind 100-foot-high protective walls—and serving their own gods.

Destined to later destroy the few northern tribes of Israel on the way to becoming an awesome world empire, these people had a reputation that was frightening. No other conquerors treated their vanquished so cruelly. They were barbaric and inhumane.

"Lord, if I do what You're requesting," Jonah might well have responded, "I'll be in a no-win situation. In the first place, it's unlikely they'll listen to any Jewish preacher. And though I don't mind jeers or a few rotten eggs, torture doesn't really appeal to me!"

You see, the Assyrians were known for ramming a sharp stake up through the chest of a prisoner, quickly planting the stake in a hole in the ground, and then laughing while the victim squirmed until dead. That was the means of execution if the prisoner was lucky. History teaches that more often than not, captives would be tied spread-eagle on the ground and slowly skinned alive!

A God Too Merciful

I can picture Jonah reminding God, "Come on, now, I have no stomach for that kind of stuff! What's that? . . . You're sure they'll listen to what I say? I can't imagine it, God. But let's just say they do, and they momentarily repent. I lose again. Because I know exactly what's going to happen. I can see it coming. Even a little godly sorrow on their part, some sniffles and a few tears, and You won't destroy them. That's it. I'm right, I know I am. I know You very well, God. You're too merciful. Your heart's too big. Do You think those people will respect You if You don't send a white blast of fire against at least a major portion of their city? Listen to me. Why be kind to them, God? They don't love You. Forget about these foreigners, they're not worth it. All they've ever given You or Your people is dirt."

So that you won't think I'm making up Jonah's thoughts, let me quote from the last chapter of this short book. Jonah had already had his whale experience. That's what finally made him willing to take on God's assignment. So he preached, and—lo and behold—the Ninevites repented in sackcloth and ashes. And, sure enough, in chapter 3, verse 10 we read: "When God saw what they did and how they turned from their evil ways, He had compassion and did not bring upon them the destruction He had threatened."

Jonah was steaming.

"But Jonah was greatly displeased and became angry. He prayed to the Lord, 'O Lord, is this not what I said when I was still at home? That is why I was so quick to flee to Tarshish. I knew that You are a gracious and compassionate God, slow to anger and abounding in love, a God who relents from sending calamity' " (Jonah 4:1-3). In other words, Jonah was telling God, "You don't treat people dirty even when that's how they act toward You. And that really frosts me!"

This account ends with God's pointing out to this prophet that "Nineveh has more than a hundred and twenty thousand people who cannot tell their right hand from their left. Should I not be concerned about that great city?" What most commentators believe this means is that there were 120,000 children in this place. So calm down, Jonah. You might just overlook that fact when you ask for judgment fire to fall, but God can't. "And yes, I love these people," the Lord was saying to Jonah. "I just wish you cared about them too."

I fear that the North American church today is quite often like Jonah. We care about our own country but not for much beyond our borders. Our spiritual dreams might include the growth of our local church and the denomination to which it belongs, but only a small percentage of Christians identify with God's great heart of love for other nations. This is especially true when we think about nations considered to be our enemies. Most believers haven't yet "broken glass" and moved into that new vista.

We may even be a bit turned off when we hear challenges based on Christ's last words. Just prior to His ascension Jesus said, "Go and make disciples of all nations . . . teaching them to obey everything I have commanded you" (Matt. 28:19-20). Apparently He wanted us to begin to think globally.

Here's how that commission comes out in Acts. "But you will receive power when the Holy Spirit comes on you: and you will be My witnesses in Jerusalem, and in all Judea and Samaria, and to the ends of the earth" (1:8). This includes places with foreign (even Assyrian-sounding) names like Mozambique, Afghanistan, Yemen, Chad, Chile, Indonesia, Somalia, Ukraine, Romania, Paraguay, Nepal, Mongolia and many more with people whose ways seem strange to us, but not to God. He loves them dearly. I didn't name one country He doesn't have intensely strong feelings for. I couldn't have named one if I'd tried.

Would you believe that it's nations other than our own where the kingdom is presently making its greatest advances? I believe it's in places foreign to us where the most exciting stories of faith are being lived out. If we remain provincial in our thinking, we are the losers. The sooner we start looking at the rest of the world, the more likely it is we will see faith being lived out in New Testament ways. So it's to our advantage to overcome the barrier of perceiving that we have all the answers, spiritually speaking.

Concern for the Innocents
We must also remember God's words to Jonah about the children, the innocents. Wherever we travel we see children. We can't just write them off. As I talk, I'm picturing the many, many children of India I've seen.

My wife, Karen, sought to help readers identify with the plight of the world's children when she wrote *Tales of the Resistance*. This is from the chapter called "The Orphan Exodus."

The orphan pavilion was to one side of the Dagoda, enclosed by a high wall with a surrounding courtyard. A sign beside the tall gate proclaimed "WE LOVE CHILDREN—Orphan Keepers' Association," but everyone in Enchanted City knew that children were loved only because they provided forced labor to do the dirty work of the Enchanter.

Two huge wolves the size of lions guarded either side of the entrance. They growled as the men approached; they bared their teeth and drooled. A soft light gathered around the King. The wolves stared, whimpered, and then hid their heads in their paws while the two men passed them by. All closed places opened to the King when he so willed it.

Inside, a squad of orphans wearing tattered rags scrubbed the courtyard. A keeper's assistant with a whistle around her neck chanted, "Clean-clean-clean!" and stood ready to beat the slow workers with a long stick. Another work detail, a long line of children tied together at the ankles with rough sections of rope, were getting ready to collect the city garbage which citizens tossed on the street. A whistle blew—*Hweet! Hweet!*— and the crew marched to the waiting carts while another assistant prodded them with the sharp tines of her forked shovel.

Huge vats of water boiled while children stirred the dirty clothes within. The hot water splashed on the orphans' rags, burning them one moment and then soaking them to the skin in the cold night. An assistant prodded them with a long wooden turning spoon. *Hweet!* she blew her whistle and shouted, "Scoundrels! Dimwits! I'll boil *you* if you spill any more wash water!"

All the orphans, boys and girls, wore the same haircuts, making it nearly impossible to tell one from another. Their clothes were an identical gray which grew increasingly threadbare during washings as they were passed down from one child to another. Skinny, sad eyed, covered with sores from the lack of proper foods, not one orphan smiled or laughed or told jokes or chased another in games of tag. Games were forbidden, and play had been outlawed. No one belonged to any other— brothers and sisters were separated. There were no holidays and never any birthday cakes.

Children are hardly the people to blame for the problems of the world. Even so, many children, through no fault of their own, live very sad lives. For example, studies show that every year more than a million children worldwide are coerced into prostitution, pornography, or other forms of sexual exploitation. The number of homeless children in the world is also in the millions.

People don't generally know that in our lifetime children in many settings have been forced to fight in adult wars. Between fifty and one hundred thousand children died in combat in the Iran/Iraq war. Sometimes these youngsters were used to clear mines. They were tied together and obliged to walk across Iraqi mine fields to detonate explosives so that the regular army could proceed unharmed.

Closer to home, reports of children being forced to fight adult wars have come out of Central American countries such as Nicaragua, Guatemala, and El Salvador.

Calling Children in Love

The Lord has a most tender heart for children. "Red and yellow, black and white, they are precious in His sight. Jesus loves the little children of the world." But many of the world's children will never hear about this love unless someone goes and tells them about our Lord. They will not grow up as my four children did, having heard about the Savior from a very early age.

I now have my first grandchild. Little Caitlyn is one year old. She's being raised in a loving Christian home and already is a regular attender at church. But millions upon millions of innocent children and grandchildren—little sons and daughters, beautiful grandsons and granddaughters—all with names and feelings and smiles and great potential for good and bad, will never hear about Christ unless someone goes to tell them the news that God and His Son, Jesus, dearly love them.

I'd like to return to the story, "The Orphan Exodus."

"I am the Orphan Keeper," she intoned. "You will do my bidding. You will keep my commands. I have control over your lives and your destinies. I am the one who says yea and nay. You can never escape. You can never go where I say no."

The children cowered, even the older ones. All knew this loveless woman had power to send them to the underworld, to poison their food and call it nightailment, to advance them or to cut off their rations. It was she who ordered punishment for all if one orphan misbehaved.

"You are mine! You are all mine!" she shouted again, lashing the air with the hand whip.

"LET MY CHILDREN GO!"

Everyone within the courtyard froze. The drums stopped in mid-roll *tatatata — TA?* Who dared disrupt the Orphan Keeper's time schedule? Who dared interrupt her early night-work-duty harangue? The children shivered in the cold, miserable with hunger and now with dread. What torture would they suffer because of this unspeakable challenge?

The King had shouted the words. He faced the Orphan Keeper, throwing the hood of his common garment back from his head as though she would recognize him once his face was fully revealed in the torchlight. The children gasped at such defiance. Who was this man?

The King's hair glimmered with gold highlights and his loosened street robe fell to the paving stones and he stood strong and tall and broad shouldered and handsome. Big Operator gasped—he had never beheld his King undisguised, so young and so beautiful.

The Orphan Keeper cracked her cat-o'nine-tails in the air. "I know you, you troublemaker. You instigator! Who do you think you are, challenging my power? The Enchanter has cast his spell over these children. They are mine! I can do what I please with them."

The King answered her not a word, but all could see he was as angry as she. He crossed the pavement and lifted his hands. A wind began to blow, around and around, *who-hooooo-ooo; who-hooooo-ooo.* It caught the torches of the torchbearers and bound the flames in one windy firebrand—*who-hooooo-ooo: who-hooooo-ooo!* Up—up!—it shot into the night sky over the orphan pavilion, blazing. By its light all could see the King grab the hand whip from the Orphan Keeper's grasp, lash the pokers from the Burners' hands, scatter the assistants with a crack, and then toss the instruments of torture to the sky. A bolt of lightning flashed from nowhere, striking with a CRA—A—A—CK! Flames burst and a ball of fire fell to the ground, finally to be extinguished at the Orphan Keeper's feet.

The ranks of orphans gasped. The assistant keepers hid their prodding spoons, sticks, and shovels behind their backs, dropped them to the ground, or pushed them under carts.

Then in the unlit dark all could see the warm radiance of the man standing in the middle of the courtyard, daring to defy the evil power of the Orphan Keeper herself. The King signaled to Big Operator and together, with a mighty thrust, they overturned the boiling vat of palace laundry. They ripped the wheels from the work carts, their muscles straining in a fury of indignation.

And no one moved to stop them. The Burners stood mesmerized. No warning signal was given to the Dagoda. The Orphan Keeper hissed as though air was escaping from her lungs—*s-s-s-s-s-s-s.*

Many of the children dropped to their knees, clasping their hands together beneath their chins, scarcely daring to hope. Was this one who could save them? Would their misery finally end? Was freedom close?

The King straightened himself again and stared the Orphan Keeper in the eyes. "You mistake yourself, madame," he said. His voice was tight with controlled wrath. "These children are not yours; they belong to me."

With those words he motioned to Big Operator, who stepped forward, wiping axle grease from his hands on his overalls. He bent his knee and bowed. Though comrade to the King before, he was an obedient subject now.

"Is the taxi vanguard ready?" asked the King.

"Yes, my Lord. Ready and waiting." His voice was full of satisfaction.

At that the Orphan Keeper screamed, staggering on her feet. "S-s-s-s. You!—you! You can't take thes-s-s-e children! They're waifs-s-s-s-s! They're cavils-s-s-s-s, slaves-s-s-s-s! The wolves-s-s-s-s will tear them to shreads-s-s-s-s. They do my bidding! They won't come with you! S-s-s-s."

Paying no attention, the King lifted his crossed arms and spread them in a circle above his head. More light diffused from his stretching embrace, till it filled every corner of the grim courtyard. The orphans' frozen feet began to warm; their cold, wet garments began to dry; their wounds and sores began to heal in the gentle light. Their hearts began to mend.

"What you don't understand, madame," said the King, "is that every orphan answers when his name is called in love."

Then the King began to call their names, names unspoken for months, for years, names they themselves had almost forgotten. He called them in family groups, brothers and sisters, brothers and brothers, sisters and sisters, according to age and position. He spoke their names with tenderness, with kindly affection, with cherished intimacy as though he had been practicing them for years.

"Kristen, Ned, James, Sara, and Susan.

Anne, Ted, John, and Linda.

Jason and Maria.

Alex, Sharon, and Rob.

Eric, Jane, and Cathy.

Diane . . ."

And each child remembered his or her name. And each child stepped from the ranks. He was more than a number, more than flesh for the meat grinder of the Enchanter's labor machines. He had a name chosen in love and a family history and a King who was worthy of service.

Can this fictional account of Christ's making children's lives easier be lived out in reality in many places of the world? I trust it's not too late to dream that this remains a possibility.

Gateway to the Heart

Children have an amazing ability to capture the hearts of adults. I recall an enchanting dirty-faced little beggar girl I encountered some years ago near the Gateway of India, Bombay's principal landmark and tourist attraction.

She could beg in I don't know how many languages. She would wait long enough to catch the language she thought you were speaking. Then she would come up and make her appeal in the few words she thought you would understand. "Money please—hungry—nice man."

I would have taken her home with me if I could. I really would have. That little lady, maybe five or six years old, found a soft-hearted American in me. I gave her money, but I often wonder what her ultimate fate was.

God's final attempt to get Jonah to identify with His concern for the great city of Nineveh was an appeal based on the 120,000 innocent children living there. Scripture doesn't say what the prophet's final response was.

I also have tried to use the appeal of children as a gateway to your heart. I hope these little ones will open modern Jonahs to the multitudes of lost folk in Nineveh-like settings foreign to us. All these people, both young and old, are God's children.

His incredible dream is to reach out to them all. And God wants us to identify both with His heart and with His command to take the message of His love to all parts of the globe. As we sing in the hymn, He wants His kingdom to spread "from shore to shore." He wants to reign "wher-e'er the sun does His successive journeys run." This is what He dares to dream.

FOR DISCUSSION AND REFLECTION

1. Grade yourself on a scale of 1 to 10 (10 being best) as to how interested you are in people of countries other than your own. Explain the reason for your mark.

2. What is a country you would like to know more about? What about that country interests you?

3. From what you have read or heard, check three of the following continents where rapid church growth is being experienced:

Africa	_____	Europe	_____
Asia	_____	North America	_____
Australia	_____	South America	_____

Compare and explain your answers.

4. Give three reasons why North American Christians should become more global in their thinking.

5. What obstacles keep you from starting to become a world-class Christian?

6. How might you benefit personally from becoming more globally aware?

READINGS

Ramji is small of stature and of dark complexion. He lives in a one-room house made of sun-baked clay. His ancestors are the aborigines of Western India. His language is an unwritten tongue called Mouchi. Ramji ekes out starvation rations for his family from a small parcel of overworked, undernourished soil which has been passed down the family line for generations. Jungle roots and occasional chunks of wild boar meat supplement the family diet.

Waghdev, the tiger god, is Ramji's tribal deity. His sincere devotion to Waghdev is astounding. Though he has never seen a Hindu hymnal, Ramji can be heard singing the praises of his deity at almost any time of the day. Though he has never read any books about Waghdev, he has an amazing wealth of information concerning him.

Ramji has never studied for the priesthood, yet he faithfully offers sacrifices to his god. He is as meticulous about the place, the time and the way in which he carries out his religious ceremonies as if he were guided by a manual of ritual. His annual blood offering (a slain chicken) is made in the hope that the tiger god will not molest his one pair of bullocks and 11 goats.

Strange, isn't it, that you have never heard of Waghdev when there are so many like Ramji who worship him so devoutly? No, it's not strange at all, for Waghdev is only a tribal deity. He is worshiped within the confines of a small geographic circle. Nor have his devotees ever dreamed of the necessity of proclaiming his virtues to others. Waghdev's responsibilities are definitely localized.

As a missionary to India, it has been my privilege to gather information on numerous tribal deities. Frankly, the more I have learned about most of them, the more thankful I've been that their influence is circumscribed. But I have become more and more concerned about one particular tribe of people. Numerically they are a much larger group than any Indian tribe of which I know. They are widely scattered and possess a great diversity of languages.

The religion of the group which concerns me has little in common with the other religions of the world. There is, however, one apparent similarity between the followers of Waghdev and this larger group; it is their indifference toward the proclaiming of the virtues of their religion to others. Let's scrutinize for a moment the religious practices of a typical devotee within this tribe and see how they compare with those of Ramji.

For the sake of convenience, let's call this fellow Anthony. Our first contact with him convinces us that he is deeply religious. He is faithful to his ritual responsibilities and sensitive to spiritual values. His religion has made a commendable contribution toward his good way of life.

But let's listen to Anthony's prayers. His requests are woven around a tight little circle of loved ones and friends. They seldom reach beyond his localized situation and never— just never across the ocean. Obviously his god is a tribal deity.

Are sacrifices and offerings a part of Anthony's worship? Indeed they are, and he is faithful in them. That is, as long as he can see some practical and personal benefit from them. If they will provide a more commodious place of worship for him, if they will lessen the amount of juvenile delinquency in his community and if they will provide schools where his children can become indoctrinated in his religion, then he is quite ready to give. In watching Anthony offer his sacrifices, one is convinced that the one who is the object of his worship is only interested in the local tribe.

It is already obvious to you that the tribe to which Anthony belongs is that large, gifted and God-blessed group of people called Christians. It is that group which has been chosen of God to be a witness of the grace of Christ to every tribe, race and nation. But Anthony, who is so typical of many in his tribe, seems as indifferent to a world without Christ as Ramji is to a world without Weghdev.

To Anthony God is bilingual, speaking only the language of heaven and English. God has no concern about getting the Gospel into other languages. God is nearsighted, seeing only the needs of men and women in the English-speaking world. God is limited in His capacity to love and partial in His desire to receive worship. He is provincial and nationalistic.

Get with It, Man, Don W. Hillis, Moody, pages 22–25.

■ ■ ■

Is missions an option — especially for super-wealthy countries like America? The biblical answer is clear. Every Christian in America has some minimal responsibility to get involved in helping the poor brethren in the church in other countries.

God has not given this superabundance of blessings to American and Canadian Christians so that we only can sit back and enjoy the luxuries of this society — or even in spiritual terms, so that we can gorge ourselves on books, teaching cassettes and deeper-life conferences. He has left us on this earth to be stewards of these spiritual and material blessings. God wants us to become experts on how to share with others.

Believers have a date with destiny. They are to be servants to the expanding churches and movement of God around the world. We need to gain a sense of trusteeship, learning to administer our wealth to accomplish the purposes of God.

What then is the bottom line? God is calling us as Christians to alter our life-styles. We must find ways to give up the non-essentials of our lives so that we can better invest our wealth in the kingdom of God.

To start, I challenge believers to lay aside at least one

dollar a day to support a native missionary in the Third World. This, of course, should be over and above our present commitments to the local church and other ministries.

I do not ask Christians to redirect their giving away from other ministries for native missions—but to expand their giving over and above current levels. Most people can do this.

For many North American and Western European believers—millions of them—this can be accomplished easily simply by giving up cookies, cakes, sweets, coffee, and other beverages. Many of these junk foods harm our bodies anyway, and anyone can save enough in this way to sponsor one or even two missionaries a month.

Many are going beyond this and, without affecting health or happiness, are able to sponsor several missionaries every month.

Of course, there are many other ways to get involved. Some cannot give more financially, but they can invest time in prayer and serve as volunteer coordinators to help recruit more sponsors. And a few ware called to go overseas to become involved experientially.

The single most important hindrance to world evangelization right now is the lack of total involvement by the body of Christ. I am convinced there are enough American and Canadian sponsors to support all the native missionaries needed to evangelize the Third World.

The Coming Revolution in World Missions, K.P. Yohannan, Creation House, pages 81–82.

■　■　■

Oswald Chambers, writer of the devotional classic *My Utmost for His Highest,* reminds us that "the basis of missionary appeals is the authority of Jesus Christ, not the needs of the heathen." In other words, we commit ourselves to growth as world-class Christians because Jesus says so in His Word, not because it is the popular or emotionally attractive thing to do.

In the mid-1980s, the world's attention turned toward the plight of famine-ravaged people in Ethiopia and the Sudan. An enormously successful concert raised millions of dollars to help alleviate the suffering. At that time, talking about the "Sahel region," discussing the injustices being done toward Eritrean people, and giving sacrificially to assist the hungry gave one admittance into the popular limelight.

Eighteen months after the concert, however, attentions had turned elsewhere. The emotional appeal of northern Africa had dissipated, and projects which had been initiated during the "boom" of giving were abandoned half-completed because the money, like the soil of these countries, had dried up.

Why? Because emotions cannot sustain the mission. They are necessary and operate effectively as catalysts, but they are not enough. Our vision for being involved as world-class Christians must be built on the sure foundation of God's Word. Our global commitment emanates out of the heart of God, not out of some popular fad of our times.

We build our vision and sustained involvement on the purposes of God as revealed in His Word.

How to Be a World-Class Christian, Paul Borthwick, Victor, pages 34–35.

■ ■ ■

It was that kind of obedience that prompted Tom and Mary Mason to agree to house an international student for the Memorial Day weekend in 1982. That was easy. The pleasant Chinese graduate student from the nearby University of Buffalo was a joy to meet. They fed him breakfast, took him to church on Sunday, and had no idea that encounter would change their lives.

Nothing much happened until the next year when they agreed to help out again. Then the local director of International Students asked Mary and her next-door neighbor, Virginia, if they'd be willing to take a group of Chinese students to Washington, D.C., for a week. Why not? Neither one of the women had ever been to the Capitol, and it sounded like an adventure. They had only three days to prepare, so they sped to the AAA for an itinerary, made lists and studied maps, and on a warm July day, the two women, plus four children and seventeen students, headed down the New York thruway in three vans.

"We literally did D.C. with a map in one hand while pointing with the other," Mary laughs when she recalls it. "We constantly got lost, but the Chinese joined in the spirit of it and had a great time."

One afternoon—Mary had planned this—they stopped in the middle of the Mall between the Washington Monument and the Lincoln Memorial and sat on the grass. Mary told the students how she had come to Jesus Christ and how He had changed her life. Then her daughter Beth played "Amazing Grace" on the violin while the students sang with them this song that was strange to them. It was a touching moment, although the students showed little response. That didn't surprise Mary. She had been told that characterized Orientals and she knew they were wary of being watched. One of them might have been—probably was—ready to report suspicious behavior to Beijing.

That fall, Mary and Virginia were invited to a Chinese dinner, a special occasion to celebrate the anniversary of the Cultural Revolution. Neither Mary nor Virginia knew before the dinner that they were the honored guests and the only Americans invited.

Toward the end of the evening, one of the Chinese women who had been on the trip to Washington pulled Mary aside and told her this story. "Do you see this little emblem I have on my lapel?" Mary nodded. It was an American flag. "Well," she said, "America will always be a special place for me. I thought about what you said in Washington and I accepted Jesus Christ as my Savior.

"I also decided I needed to make some changes in my life. I had come to this country to stay. We have been slowly getting our family out of China and only my husband is left there. He is a high government official and can't leave yet. But now that I'm a Christian, my son has become a Christian, and we've decided to go home and share the Word with our family and our country."

"It was enough," says Mary, "to keep me going for years."

And keep going for years she has. The Masons began to host students for a week or two weeks at a time—mostly Japanese or Chinese. Then Mary began teaching English as a second language and holding Bible studies in her home. The latest was a Monday morning study made up of six Korean men and women.

One day when Gordon Loux visited the Masons, Tom hit the playback button on his telephone answering machine. A woman with a Japanese accent left a message that told it all: "Hi, Mom and Dad! Just called to say I love you. No need to call back."

The Masons will never know while on this earth how many lives they have influenced and in what way. That's true for most of us. Scrapbooks are crammed with stories of one person who got an idea or got mad or got unwittingly involved in a cause and ended up changing a community, or preserving the environment or saving lives.

You Can Be a Point of Light, Gordon Loux and Ronald L. Wilson, Multnomah, pages 21–23.

■ ■ ■

God has called us to prayer for "all nations." There is no better way than starting at the top.

The other day a friend asked me to write a few words of explanation on the theme "How to pray for world leaders."

As I worked to keep the guidelines brief, I was forced to simply give Scripture references at points where fully developed teachings would be completely appropriate. If you take time with your Bible and the following suggestions, I believe your effectiveness in prayer will deepen.

First: Be convinced that God has placed these leaders in their positions. As to whether they have ruled in evil or righteousness, they will give account, but it is God's sovereignty that has ordained their term of governing nonetheless (Romans 13:1-4).

Second: It is the believer's responsibility to pray for all governmental leaders. Our calling is not to pass judgment on their rule; but, in obedience to God's Word, to enter into prayer with intercessions that order and peace may fill each land (1 Timothy 2:1, 2).

Third: Such praying makes possible the rise of righteous rule in any land, for God OVERrules in all things when intercessory prayer prevails (Psalm 75:7-10). Further, such praying pleases God, for it paves the way for fruitful evangelism to take place in each nation (1 Timothy 2:3-4).

Fourth: Let your heart be filled with confidence that prayer will introduce God's overruling hand wherever faithful believers call forth His dominion. "Your will be done on earth as it is in heaven," is a prayer Jesus taught us to pray *now* (Matthew 6:10).

Fifth: Pray for national leaders to be taught by God that the Lord Almighty is the source of their rule. Pray that humility will fill the hearts of kings who learn to fear God (Daniel 4:34-35). Pray that leaders will love their people more than they love themselves; that they will serve as shepherds and not as taskmasters (Micah 6:8; Jeremiah 23:4, 5).

Finally: Pray for the family of each national leader. God is able to work wonders in the heart of any man or woman at this practical dimension of daily life. Rightly ordered authority begins in the home—in family relationships. Pray for miracles in the households of world leaders (Philippians 4:22).

It's astounding to realize that we live in an era of almost instant global communication. As children of our heavenly Father, however, we possess something even more astounding: instant communication with the One who made the world and knows the hearts of all its rulers.

Moments with Majesty, Jack Hayford, Multnomah, pages 158–59.

CHAPTER FIVE

CONFRONT THE SCANDAL OF OUR PREJUDICES

Maybe you're like I am. Every so often you have a dream that really troubles you. For example, here's a recurring nightmare of mine I recall from years back. I would be watching from the last row of an auditorium as a magician performed illusions. He would ask for a volunteer to come up, and one of my young sons, who was sitting down in front would respond. He would be put in a box through which a sword was to be thrust. But suddenly I knew the trick wasn't going to work, and my son would actually be killed. So I'd race to the front, trying to stop things, but I would always be too late. I'd hear a piercing scream, at which point I'd wake up, terrified.

Usually I don't remember my dreams. But I had this one more than once, and it was troubling enough to remember.

I'm told that one's dreams are usually not about somebody else, like my young son, but about oneself. With that perspective, I eventually became aware that this dream was underscoring what God had been telling me through a number of different means. There were little-boy aspects of my personality that needed to be put to death. If I didn't stop acting like a little boy in some ways, the Lord would never be able to entrust me with certain adult assignments. I feel I've heeded those warnings from the Lord and done the work He wanted accomplished. And, interestingly, that dream hasn't returned.

Confronted by the Lord

In Scripture, we see that Peter had one of these unusual revelations from the Lord while he was in Joppa.

> About noon the following day as they were approaching the city, Peter went up on the roof to pray. He became hungry and wanted something to eat, and while the meal was being prepared, he fell into a trance. He saw heaven opened and something like a large sheet being let down to earth by its four corners. It contained all kinds of four-footed animals, as well as reptiles of the earth and birds of the air. Then a voice told him, "Get up, Peter. Kill and eat."
>
> "Surely not, Lord!" Peter replied. "I have never eaten anything impure or unclean."
>
> The voice spoke to him a second time, "Do not call anything impure that God has made clean."
>
> This happened three times, and immediately the sheet was taken back to heaven. . . .
>
> While Peter was still thinking about the vision, the Spirit said to him, "Simon, three men are looking for you. So get up and go downstairs. Do not hesitate to go with them, for I have sent them."
>
> Peter went down and said to the men, "I'm the one you're looking for. Why have you come?" (Acts 10:9-16, 19-21)

It was then he learned they had been sent by a Gentile named Cornelius, a centurion in what was called the Italian regiment. "He is a righteous and God-fearing man, who is respected by all the Jewish people," they said. "A holy angel told him to have you come to his house so that he could hear what you have to say" (v. 22).

The Lord was preparing Peter to be responsive to the invitation of this Gentile he normally wouldn't even have associated with. That's because God wanted His apostles to extend the message of His kingdom beyond the Jewish world. To do that, to get these servants of His to buy into His more expansive dream, the Lord had to somehow break through certain prejudices they held.

Peter figured out the puzzle of his vision a lot faster than I did the message of my dream. He had to, because before long he found himself at the home of Cornelius, preaching Christ and seeing the Holy Spirit fall upon the group. The Scriptures report:

> While Peter was still speaking these words, the Holy Spirit came on all who heard the message. The circumcised believers [or, the Jewish believers] who had come with Peter were astonished that the gift of the Holy Spirit had been poured out even on the Gentiles. For they heard them speaking in tongues and praising God (Acts 10:44-46).

I believe it's fair to say that God forces us to confront the scandal of our prejudices when they stand in the way of the fulfillment of His dreams. The early church, which was almost exclusively Jewish, would undoubtedly have stayed that way if the Lord had not pushed His key leaders, such as Peter, and said, "Don't call anything impure that God has made clean."

Since the first century, this kind of nudging has continued through the generations. I hold the conviction that this is one of the things the Lord is trying to do in His church even today.

Double Bind

I've illustrated previous chapters with sections from *Tales of the Resistance,* written by my wife, Karen. Her tale called "Doubletalk, Triple Tongue, and Theysay" has something to teach us about prejudice.

> Heralds stood on broadcast columns throughout Enchanted City and shouted news. They announced special events as well as the hour of the night. Because of power-outs, however, no one really knew the correct time. One herald might proclaim, "Midnight. All's well!" while another shouted "Ten thirty o'clock. Half-night

approaches!" No wonder citizens suffered from indigestion, they were always eating dinner at the wrong hour.

Doubletalk, Triple Tongue, and Theysay were friends. The three boys had grown up in Moire Oxan, the tenement slums which stretched for miles, hovel stacked upon hovel. Together they endured illness, poverty, hunger, and branding. When Theysay's parents died, the other two helped him escape orphan dragnets by hiding him back and forth in their own tenement hovels, at great risk of penalty to themselves.

All were now heralds of the Enchanter—and proud of their accomplishment. It was something for penniless young men to rise to heraldship, to stand on the tall broadcast columns, trusted with all the news fit to proclaim. It was something for ragtag ruffians to wear the red and yellow jerseys with the Enchanter's insignia of blazing fire. It was something to blow the herald horn whenever the wizard's sleek black limousine moved ominously through the city streets, and to shout, "The Enchanter is coming! Make way for the Enchanter!"

Unfortunately, heralds frequently made contradictory announcements. One might shout, "Melons in the marketplace! First come, first served!" while the herald on the very next post was shouting, "No melons today! Try rutabagas in your fruit salad!"

Some people suspected that heralds were chosen only if they had something wrong with their speech. Some heralds spoke backwards, "!gnimoc si retnahcnE ehT" Some had twisted tongues. Some had lockmouth, so that all s's whistled through clenched teeth with a wicked his-s-s-s-s-s. Some had very bad breath.

Doubletalk made positive announcements out of one side of his mouth. "The Enchanter is coming!", for instance, or, "Melons in the marketplace!" would be announced out of the right side. Negative announcements, however, would be shouted out of the left side of his mouth: "The Enchanter is not coming!" "The melons have all been stolen!"

Trouble began when Doubletalk couldn't decide if the

announcement was negative or positive. Was the theft of rutabagas good or bad news? Or, maybe, it was a good thing that the Enchanter wasn't coming.

Consequently, he began to make announcements out of both sides of his mouth. "The Enchanter is coming!" (on the right side). "The Enchanter is not coming!" (on the left). Then both at the same time. His tongue worked so hard it eventually split in two.

Doubletalk always worked up a sweat, but no one appreciated his great effort. People standing beneath his column shouted, "Heh, bub! Make up yer mind. Watcha got? Wet-noodle brains?" And they threw rotten tomatoes.

Double talk — one thing out of one side of the mouth and something else out of the other side. Contradictory announcements.

— Witness to your non-Christian friends, but don't associate with too many non-Christians or you might compromise your convictions.

— Treat all people with Christian love — except African Americans who move into your neighborhood, because then your property value will drop.

— Make use of all the gifts the Holy Spirit has given you — unless, of course, you are a woman who would violate all that is sacred if you thought you had gifts intended only for men.

Prejudices. We still have them, don't we? I see them often standing in the way of the dreams God has for the world.

Personal Cram Course

Have you ever tried to master some difficult subject by taking a cram course? Perhaps in a short period of time you were going to learn how to speak French or become an accomplished pianist.

What happened?

I could say I took a twelve-year inner city cram course on racial reconciliation. Now for some, twelve years might seem too long for a cram course. But when we realize that racism in this land has been hundreds of years in the making, twelve years is actually rather a short period of time in which to expect to master the subject!

What happened was that I founded an inner city, interracial church that which quickly grew to a Sunday morning attendance of 500. On my staff were a Chinese Filipino man, an African American man, and also a white woman. We did well, for a while—about eight years. But eventually all the blacks left. I confess that I, as senior minister, was as much involved and to blame for what happened as anyone. In retrospect, I would say I flunked the racial reconciliation course. On the other hand, I certainly learned a great deal, probably as much about my flaws as anything! So when I talk about personal racism or racism in the church, it's not just another topic to me.

That church ministry began in 1967. At that time in Chicago there was minimal communication between the black church and the white church. Today, in this third largest of U.S. cities, there are ministries where blacks and whites work together in the church beautifully. I applaud those efforts. In fact, I stand and applaud. I rejoice. I shout, "Praise the Lord!"

But the truth is, when you look at the broader church picture, not much progress has been made toward racial reconciliation. When it comes to blacks and whites working together, the church lags behind the sports world, the entertainment world, the world of education, the world of business, the world of government, and on and on.

There's a strong white church, there's a strong black church, and there's a strong Hispanic church. But there isn't nearly as much of a coming together racially as we might like to think. Most honest church leaders would say that as Christians we're probably fifteen to twenty years behind where we should be on this issue.

Don't misunderstand. I'm not equating the church with the Ku Klux Klan. I'm not overlooking the fact that some progress has been made. I'm just honestly pointing out that Christians should be a lot farther along than we are in terms of racial reconciliation.

Most churches or parachurch organizations are not in a

position to boast. More likely, they admit to finding the race issue an extremely difficult problem to work through. But if Christians ever expect to be heard as a viable voice in Chicago or in this nation or in North America, then racism in the church must be addressed. It's a glass ceiling that needs to be shattered, and soon.

My conviction is that God still forces His people to confront the scandal of their prejudices when they stand in the way of His dreams becoming reality. As we plead with the Spirit for revival *in the church,* I believe this is one of the sins He will convict us of. Daring to dream again means breaking through the racial barriers that hold us back.

Getting Together

Another prejudice that needs to be addressed is our denominationalism. I'm not necessarily advocating that we join together as part of a great ecumenical movement. We don't need to blindly embrace the minister down the street who believes Christ to be a good man but little more—and certainly not the unique Son of God. There are essential doctrinal differences that cannot be overlooked.

But that doesn't mean that all in the true body of Christ, those who have received His saving grace, can't learn to work together better. In our land the enemy is increasing in power. The strides Satan has made in recent years are frightening. Christians will never stop him if we can't learn to cooperate more.

I am thrilled with reports I hear of ministers in many parts of the country praying together across denominational lines. We are not as far behind denominationally as we are racially, but that's hardly a high compliment.

As I talk with church leaders, I am amazed how little Baptists know about Episcopalians, or Episcopalians about the Salvation Army, or the Army about what's happening in Presbyterian circles. In many ways these are like different worlds which seldom interface unless something like a Billy Graham Crusade brings them together.

In a given town, churches and the people of those various churches so often are spiritually isolated from one another.

Free Methodists don't know who attends the local Church of God church, or the Missouri Synod Lutheran church, or the Evangelical Free church, or the Assembly of God church. There are exceptions, but on the whole we don't really know the true body of Christ in our particular settings as I believe our Lord would like us to.

Are times changing? I hope so. It's never too late to dream. But, I wonder, will minor differences or our fears of one another continue to keep us apart so that we'll never know how strong we could have been, if only we had worked harder at being unified?

Let's face the facts. It still befuddles the average non-Christian that the church has so many divisions. If Christians agree on the greater portion of their beliefs, why don't they concentrate on that rather than on their differences? Let's wake up. Our divisions absolutely bamboozle nonbelievers! We Christians should be equally concerned.

I have preached in many different denominational settings. I've never yet found a group I didn't like, never! Mennonites, Wesleyans, Nazarenes, Friends, Moravians, they're all wonderful people. Lord, bring us together!

I believe He wants to do just that. I truly am convinced God is almost forcing us to confront this scandal of our denominational prejudices, because it stands in the way of His dreams for us becoming reality.

There are so many Scriptures which speak to issues like these. In 1 Corinthians 1, the Apostle Paul writes: "One of you says, 'I follow Paul'; another, 'I follow Apollos'; another, 'I follow Cephas'; still another, 'I follow Christ.' Is Christ divided?" Paul asks in wonderment! (vv. 12-13)

Sharing the Burden

A passage like John 4 reveals the racism of New Testament times as we see the Samaritan woman responding to Christ, "How can You ask me for a drink?" John, the author adds in parentheses: "(for Jews do not associate with Samaritans)." But Jesus did anyway (v. 9).

Also revealing is verse 27 of that chapter. When the disciples returned to the scene, the Scriptures record, they were surprised, not that Jesus was talking to a Samaritan, but that our Lord was conversing with a woman!

I believe we still have lessons to learn from Christ on this matter. In Luke 8, referring to Jesus' travels from one town and village to another, we read, "The Twelve were with Him, and also some women" (vv. 1-2). The passage names three of them: Mary Magdalene, Susanna, and Joanna. Joanna's husband, Cuza, was the manager of Herod's household. So the wife of the king's steward was traveling with Jesus as He preached!

According to Luke 8:3, "These women were helping to support them [the disciples] out of their own means." Ministry requires money, and apparently a lot of it was being provided by the women who traveled with Christ.

Contrary to the practices of the day, Jesus opened up places of service like this for women. It was risky. There could have been a lot of misunderstandings about women traveling with His ministry team. But Jesus didn't exclude them. I believe we too need to open up more places for women to use their special resources for kingdom work.

With that statement I haven't tried to resolve all the doctrinal issues related to women in ministry. But I am challenging men of the church to make more room at the table for women, just as we need to do for minorities. Can you respond "amen" to that?

For too long we have stereotyped women as being capable of taking charge of the church nursery but not the church treasury. We've said women can teach boys and girls, but not a mixed adult class. In Scripture we read that women should learn in silence. Often the only word we see is "silence." We miss the fact that women were encouraged to inquire and learn. Why learn if one's knowledge can't be used?

One of the great unsung demonstrations of the working of the Holy Spirit in the church in our land is what's happening among women. They are becoming "maiden warriors." I commend my sisters in the Lord. And I believe the Lord is challenging many of us who are men to confront the scandal of our sexual prejudices.

This chapter has been a cram course. I've tried to write too much in too restricted a space. Suffice it to underscore that this matter of prejudices is a real-life nightmare that continues to trouble the church. The Lord is telling me to grow up and stop acting out of little-boy fears. What's He saying to you?

FOR DISCUSSION AND REFLECTION

1. Are there prejudices in the North American church that still grieve the heart of God? If so, what are they?

2. Sincere Christians sometimes reinforce their prejudices by appealing to Scripture. How is this possible?

3. In an effort to overcome prejudice and show love and understanding, Christians can sometimes compromise what Scripture teaches. Give an example of how this might happen.

4. Who are people or groups you have prejudged or were prejudiced toward in the past?

5. Has the Holy Spirit been revealing any new prejudices you need to correct? What has God been showing you?

6. When it comes to tearing down walls of prejudice, is the church in North America ahead of or behind the secular culture? Why?

READINGS

Director Spike Lee's movie *Malcolm X* hit the theaters in 1992, spawning a revival of the Black Muslim leader's controversial and powerful rhetoric of the sixties (not to mention X hats and tee shirts sprouting from coast to coast). In one scene in the movie, a white coed approaches Malcolm X as he arrives on the campus of Harvard University to give a speech. She assures him that even though she's white, she's sympathetic to his cause.

"What can someone like me do to help?" she asks earnestly.

"Nothing," he answers coldly.

Part of Malcolm X's great appeal to the black community was that he stood up for black self-determination. He challenged blacks to stay in school, get off drugs, get off welfare, get a job, and take responsibility for their families. But unlike Martin Luther King, Jr., who walked hand in hand with whites as he challenged the American conscience, Malcolm's message—at that time—was: "We don't need whites to make it." Many blacks still believe that. They desire independence and disdain whites as controllers.

In the realm of Christian fellowship and effective growth in the church, many still believe blacks and whites can go their independent ways and remain effective. In the mid-'80s, C. Peter Wagner of the Church Growth Institute at Fuller Theological Seminary in Pasadena, California, published two books discussing the factors that characterize growing churches. One of the more controversial principles growing out of the Institute's research is the homogeneous factor—that is, people feel most comfortable with people like themselves; therefore, churches must take this human tendency into account if they wish to draw in new members.

Wagner is partially correct; the human tendency is to seek those like ourselves. "Birds of a feather do flock together," and when it comes to church, Christians generally sort themselves out by race, class, and culture. It's not only black and white, either. Most Georgia farmers would feel quite out of place in a highbrow Episcopal service; Cambodian refugees are forming their own congregations under the umbrella of a sponsoring American church; Spanish-speaking and Korean congregations feel the need to preserve their distinctiveness.

Do we need each other? Those who believe in "homogeneous churches" and "niche marketing" or Afro-centrism and self-determination don't necessarily think so. Other than trying to avoid race riots, why should we go through all the grief necessary to achieve racial reconciliation? Why fight human nature? Why not just let "them" have their church, and "we" will have our church?

The real question, however, is do we solidify the human tendency to flock together with our own kind into a "principle" for the body of Christ? Do we accept a "separate but equal" mind-set for Christian fellowship and relationship?

Our answer is no. We cannot get along without each other if the body of Christ is to be salt and light to a world torn apart by racial strife. The principle of interdependence recognizes our differences but realizes that we each bring something to the table that the other person needs, resulting in equality (key verses: 2 Corinthians 8:12-14). Interdependence demonstrates the transforming nature of the gospel and declares that we do need each other if we are to live out the ministry of reconciliation. (Where would the gospel be today if Christ's disciples throughout the centuries had not accepted His challenge to be ambassadors of reconciliation across racial and cultural barriers?)

Breaking Down Walls, Raleigh Washington and Glen Kehrein, Moody, pages 169–71.

■ ■ ■

The bottom line is that the church is still the most segregated community in America. We have not found each other, except on the annual rent-a-choir day. So a moratorium on church growth for the purpose of majoring in reconciliation might not be such a bad idea. The witness it would show to a confused society grappling for ways to mend broken fences could just result in the greatest growth the church has witnessed in quite a while.

The impression I get from my colleagues in psychology, pastoral care, and counseling is that reconciliation is hard work. It requires confrontation, getting beyond mere words to true feelings and attitudes, many of which we may not even be aware. Of course, this presumes we must be in the same room together. Beyond that, it requires setting up listening posts where we can speak with one another about the things that have kept us apart. The church ought to be such a listening post. This must become the preoccupation of the church's leadership. Unless it does, the church will be mute before the ravages of on-going racial and ethnic animosity.

I believe that the future of human relations in our cities is ultimately in the hands of churches. It is here where politicians, cops, citizen-victims of police brutality, business leaders, moms and pops from those small stores—all sorts of people—could meet to talk, perchance to pray. Some fine ministry work is already being done among urban gangs, but gang members are regarded as the scum of the earth by too many people in too many churches. We need to view these wandering youths as "sheep . . . scattered . . . without a shepherd." (Who will mediate between these gang members and the local police precinct? Probably not the police chaplain—

he is too much of a cop himself or he wouldn't be accepted by the establishment. The answer might emerge if community-based policing becomes fully operative. Then cops might get names, and gang members faces. But until that happens, and even after it does, the church has an important role to play.

_____

The Coming Race Wars? William Pannell, Zondervan, pages 138–39.

■ ■ ■

I am a graduate of four distinctly conservative institutions — Bob Jones University, Reformed Episcopal Seminary, Covenant Theological Seminary, and Concordia Theological Seminary. I am also a professor of theology at Wheaton College and Graduate School, an evangelical institution known for its conservative point of view.

As you might expect, I have been decidedly influenced by my experiences at these various institutions and the church groups they represent. And, as the philosopher Hans-Georg Gadamer would say, I carry around within me these influences as well as influences from home and from life in general. Gadamer calls these experiences "prejudices." I have, you might say, a conditioning within me that I cannot completely overcome; I hold prejudices from such diverse sources as fundamentalism, Calvinism, Lutheranism, and evangelicalism. These points of view influence the way I think about the Christian faith and the way I worship.

All of us—and our churches—have dispositions of this sort. It's not that we are intentionally prejudiced. Instead, the environments in which we were raised and in which we have worshiped build within us convictions that we may not even be able to identify.

For example, the nonliturgical background of my early years naturally made me skeptical about both the liturgical and charismatic traditions of worship. I was suspicious of anyone who did not believe or practice the Christian faith as I did. And I was dead certain that I was right and they were wrong.

These prejudices became ingrained during my years at

home and my formative years in college. I can point to an incident when I was twelve years old that surely built prejudice within me. The story goes like this: A Reformed couple came to our Baptist parsonage to visit with my parents. As they were deeply engaged in conversation about some religious matter—the favorite topic in my home—the male visitor lighted a cigarette right there in our living room. I was shocked. How could someone talk about religion and smoke at the same time?

As soon as our guests left, I quickly made my way to my mother's side. "Mother, I thought those people were Christians. How can somebody smoke and be a Christian?" My mother's answer was classic: "Well, Robert, they are Reformed. And Reformed people, though they are Christian, have funny ideas and do worldly things. But we are Baptists, the best of the Christian groups. We don't have funny ideas and aren't worldly." Right then and there, in that young and impressionable mind, a prejudice was set in place.

I had similar experiences in college. I can, for example, distinctly remember the founder of the college cupping his hands over his mouth in chapel and crying, "Do you want to know where a man stands with God?" Obviously anyone who is spiritually sensitive wants to know how to determine a person's standing with God. I leaned forward, anxiously awaiting his answer. "You only have to ask that person one question," he continued. Then, after a moment's pause, came the confident, dogmatic assertion, "Ask him, 'What do you think of this university?'"

Now I was aware of how people felt about that university. Some thought the school was reactionary, racist, legalistic, dogmatic, and arrogant. "What about those people?" I thought. "Is God angry with them? Have they really fallen away from the truth?" As I recalled other assertions I'd heard proclaimed at the college, I found myself asking, "Is everybody in the World Council of Churches an apostate renegade seeking to destroy the true church? Are all liturgical people really ritualists, servants of a dead orthodoxy given to vain repetition? Is the charismatic movement really of the devil?" With all of these questions, I was dealing with prejudices that had long ago been planted in my mind like seeds placed in the rich, dark soil of a spring garden.

Signs of Wonder, Robert Webber, Abbott Martyn, pages 6–7.

■ ■ ■

A good portion of my life has been given to a teaching ministry that has taken me all over the country and Canada. In a way, I come alive when I take my place before an audience. I work hard to be a conscientious communicator. I pray fervently, and I am often gratified by obvious effectiveness. However, there are many men who have made it a point not to be present when I speak.

Pastors introduce me for conferences in their buildings and then mysteriously absent themselves from the auditorium. In a missions-emphasis week in a church in the South, the entire male staff, after welcoming the audience and greeting me, slipped out the side doors. Friends of mine, finer speakers than me, have endured the indignity of rows of men demonstrating their disapproval by pointedly exiting as they spoke. Women editors often support me when I speak at publishing conventions, but the male executives of publishing enterprises rarely show, even when I'm sponsored by their houses. When I'm a plenary speaker at a major convention, other speakers (almost always all men) are too busy, schedule committee meetings, or catch late suppers. Sometimes I receive apologetic excuses, but most of the time significant men are conspicuous by their absence.

"How does this all make you feel?" asked a friend who is a clinical counselor. For years, I didn't think anything about male support (or its lack), but after a while there began to be a cumulative negative impact. "Well," I replied to my counselor friend, "it makes me feel as though I am not considered a ministering peer, that I am not important enough to give thirty or forty minutes to hear. It makes me feel as though I am not worthy of professional courtesy."

I have been mute about the discourtesy, accepted it as my lot as a woman, been careful not to speak in situations where the spiritual leadership is uncomfortable with extending an invitation to a woman. ("What does your pastor think about my speaking?" I inquire. "Your church governing board?") I have attempted not to become indignant.

The next day, another phone call from my rector—an additional thought. Then in the afternoon, a formal handwritten note of commendation arrives in the mail. These affirmations thrust me again into painful emotion. My soul is sliced open by kindness, and I cannot staunch the weeping.

Lonely No More, Karen Burton Mains, Word, pages 82–83.

■ ■ ■

The needs, potential, and qualifications of women have been shrouded in the mists of interminable squabbles about women's roles in the church. Whatever your view about these matters, our fights have done nothing to erase the deeply ingrained prejudices of men toward women. We cannot continue our rather brutish behavior, thinking that our patient Christian wives, friends, and fellow workers don't really care. We mistakenly assume that because they are not radical feminists they have no feelings.

Change begins with our language, because what we say and what we write reveals our unchallenged assumptions about women. Beyond that, however, we must change our missions commitment to include evangelizing and training the world's women. Women leaders from Africa and Asia have correctly exposed the blind side of church and mission strategies in this regard. If we contemplate new ministries, without taking into account the huge potential for significant leadership among Christian women, we enter the field with one arm cut off.

Too often we act as if missions history means nothing. How many times do we ring the changes on William Carey, Hudson Taylor, and Jim Elliot, without ever mentioning Mary Slessor, Gladys Aylward, and Helen Roseveare. What does such oversight say to women in our schools and churches? If mission work sounds like the private domain of an exclusive men's club, we aren't going to attract capable women.

Perhaps the strongest signal we send women in the role we give, or do not give, to them in mission leadership. Some of our institutions would be better served if the wives of the men in charge were given the job. In these cases, the wife is gifted in management and administration, while her husband's gifts are in teaching, preaching, and counseling. The point is to use people in their strengths, regardless of their sex. The work of God could be considerably expedited if we got serious about developing women for leadership in world missions.

Men, it's long past the time to change.

James Reapsome, "Men: It's Time to Change," *Pulse*, 9 October 1991. Used by permission.

CHAPTER SIX

EMPOWER OUR ACTIVITIES WITH PRAYER

Do impossible dreams ever come true? The answer to that question is, yes they do! Especially they do if we involve God in what's taking place and don't just rely on our own resources.

Let me illustrate with stories of two persistent women and what God did for each of them. The key to their success, I believe, is this: There's always a better chance that an impossible dream will come true if the person involved shows why it's to God's advantage to help bring it about.

One of the stories comes from the Old Testament. This woman was in a bad home setting, in a bad religious setting, and she had a bad history of humiliation. Her name was Hannah. She was married to Elkanah, but unfortunately she wasn't this gentleman's only wife. The good news is that she was his favorite. Her bad news is that she was barren. But it wasn't too late for her to dream.

The Scriptures report that year after year Elkanah went up from his town to worship and sacrifice to the Lord Almighty at Shiloh, where Hophni and Phinehas, the two sons of Eli, were priests of the Lord. We know these two guys were bad news. Hophni and Phinehas were wicked. The religious scandals we've known in our day are nothing compared to the shenanigans of these brothers.

The Bible declares they had no regard for the Lord. They

were having sex with the women who served at the entrance of the Tent of Meeting, and in strong-arm fashion they were stealing all the meat they wanted from those who brought animals for sacrifice. As priests, these men totally disregarded the prescribed religious ceremonial rules.

Year of the Miracle

In God's providence, however (this is a marvelous God Hunt sighting), the "year of the miracle" for Hannah took place when Eli, the wicked priests' father, was serving. That meant someone with spiritual sensitivity would witness what was about to happen. First Samuel, chapter 1 reveals that Hannah was "in bitterness of soul." Her rival wife had provoked her until she wept and couldn't eat. This verbal abuse came because Hannah didn't seem to be able to have children. Verses 10-11 read:

> In bitterness of soul Hannah wept much and prayed to the Lord. And she made a vow, saying, "O Lord Almighty, if You will only look upon Your servant's misery and remember me, and not forget Your servant but give her a son, then I will give him to the Lord for all the days of his life."

It's precisely at this point that Hannah did something special. Whether it was conscious or unconscious, I can't say, but she allowed her desires to overlap the desires of God. Frequently our praying is just for selfish ends. But, praise the Lord, Hannah had stumbled onto something when she made this vow.

At first Eli thought she was drunk. That's because her agony was so great. But she sobbed, "Not so, my lord . . . I am a woman who is deeply troubled. I have not been drinking wine or beer; I was pouring out my soul to the Lord. . . . I have been praying here out of my great anguish and grief" (vv. 15-16).

To this, Eli prophetically responded, "Go in peace, and may the God of Israel grant you what you have asked of Him" (v. 17). Verse 20 is where we see that the impossible dream came true: "So in the course of time Hannah conceived and gave birth to a son." The meaning of her son's name was "because I asked the Lord for him." Hannah hadn't forgotten her divine bargain. "Because I asked the Lord for him," put into a word, is the name Samuel. And Samuel was to be a remarkable person from the time he was a young lad all the way through old age, always being faithful to his Heavenly Master.

Again, the secret revealed here is that Hannah had taken her impossible request to the Lord, and in doing so she had leveraged, if you will, how it would be to God's advantage to grant her petition.

Often, I believe, the impossible dreams we dream would really be of little advantage to God were He to respond in the way we ask. Think about some of the prayer requests you've heard (or offered) recently. How well do they reflect God's kingdom goals?

Overlapping Desires

A second example of a woman who allowed her desires to overlap God's dreams is the fictional character Amanda. This story comes from *Tales of the Resistance.*

At first, Amanda came to the courtyard simply because she needed a rest from the stress of traffic dispatching. Now she came because the plight of the girl drew her, a plight she didn't understand.

One night a damp fog stinking of sludge smoke and burning garbage settled on the city. Amanda walked the dark streets, restless for clean air and the sun and a romp on spongy moss. She was not afraid to roam at night. Amanda was not afraid of anything, except her own dangerous stubbornness—a lesson hard learned in a terrible incident which had brought shame to herself, pain to all she loved, and disaster to the only place she would ever call home.

She had loved a forbidden thing and had not been the same child since. A child with wild flowers in her hair, whose laughter constantly announced her presence,

Amanda once had loved extravagantly, without question. Now she questioned all loves and was cautious about loving anything.

On this night Amanda slipped into the courtyard. The lanterns cast an eerie glimmer in the fog which oozed from the streets under the heavy outer doors. She stood beneath the balcony window, glad that the girl would not have to make many appearances on this frightful night.

The bell whispered—oh, dear, she had gazed too long. The girl appeared; Amanda was sorry to have disturbed her. "She's very beautiful," said a voice from the shadows behind her.

Amanda whirled around! Who was hiding in the courtyard?

"Don't be afraid—" the form moved away from the cloisters. Even in the damp fog, its motion was familiar. The voice was comforting, a well-known voice.

Her old impudence returned. "Have you nothing better to do than frighten unsuspecting maidens in dark streets? I thought you were supposed to be out chronicling Sightings." But Amanda was glad to see her old friend. Though she had heard much about his exploits, their paths had not crossed since that first day's encounter in the taxi terminal.

Hero spoke in a low voice. "The same old Amanda. Be careful what you say. Anyone (or anything) may be hiding in the shadows. This is a bastion of the Enchanter."

He lifted a lantern from its hook and carefully shone it in the corners. They were alone. The girl on the balcony had taken her bored silence inside.

He was taller than she remembered. By the light of the lantern she noticed that the planes and angles of his face had broadened, outgrowing the scar which had disfigured a boy's cheek. Now the old wound gave him a rakish, elegant air. He had become handsome.

She wanted to protest, "I'm *not* the same old Amanda. I'm no longer just a play friend!" But she suspected he had grown so tall he would never notice that she had grown as well.

He pulled her to a bench, where they sat together. "Big Operator told me that you come here often." He spread his dark blue slicker around her shoulders to shelter her from the damp. Its color reminded her of the soft, rich homespun of Ranger cloaks, of flashing silver insignias, of courage and proud command and of the forest cry, "The Kingdom comes!"

"Amanda, you need to be careful roaming through Enchanted City. Great dangers lurk in every corner of every street."

Amanda stiffened. Her answer was also low. "I can take care of myself."

But Hero was in earnest. "In Great Park you are the amazing princess who used to outspit and outaim any contenders! But this is my territory. Innocence is dangerous in Enchanted City. Case in point: Don't ever come out on rainy nights without a covering, some sort of macintosh. Even the air bodes ill; people die of the nightailment. The health you take for granted in Great Park, the healing powers of Mercie are not natural to this place."

Amanda felt an old indignation rise—she was not a child—but just as suddenly it slipped away. She had learned all too well the folly of arrogance. She *had* been cold. She *was* glad for the warmth of his shared rain cloth. He was right, the paths and forest trails were her native terrain; but the hard paving stones of this dark place were his. Now she must learn from him.

The courtyard doors to the street creaked open. A form crept in and Amanda felt Hero tense beside her and grasp the handle of the hatchet beneath his slicker. A Breaker had entered the courtyard. Amanda's own heart quickened; she had once seen the chalky white face, the piercing eyes, the chilling grin, the cudgel raised to bash her as she lay in pain. *To the King,* she mentally intoned. *To the Restoration.* The bell whispered; the girl came to the balcony; the Breaker gazed and withdrew to the streets.

Hero murmured again, "She's so beautiful even the no-people come to look."

"But her eyes, her eyes—they're blank. There's no life in them."

"Of course," explained Hero. "She's the Forbidden Princess."

"The Forbidden Princess?" Amanda asked. They were out on the street now, walking back to the Taxi Company.

City wise, the young man told her the story of the beautiful girls gathered together every year to serve as temple keepers for the Enchanter. Chosen for their courage as well as for their beauty, a terrible initiation separated those who were worthy from those who were only fair. The novitiates spent a night in a room with severed bulls' heads. Those who didn't weep or whine were chosen to become princesses who spent the rest of their young lives allowing the curious to gaze on their faces, but forbidden to speak to any admirers.

"How awful!" said Amanda.

"That's not all. Eventually they become wives to the Enchanter. The children they bear are the Enchanter's elite guard, Burners and Breakers, the no-people. The Enchanter has had thousands of wives. Most of them shrivel and waste away—heartsickness. His embrace is so terrible that even beauty and courage are not protection enough."

They stood talking before the overhead garage door of the City Taxi Company and waited for a cab to return rather than bother a mechanic. Sometimes, in the rain, the city was almost beautiful the way the lights danced on the wet stones. A taxi beeped its horn, the crank creaked inside, the door slid upwards.

"Amanda?" Hero placed a hand on her shoulder. "Don't go to the temple courtyard so often. It's dangerous. There's nothing you can do for the princess, and Big Operator says your work as a dispatcher is invaluable. Hundreds have been helped because of your quick gifts of seeing and aiming."

Amanda watched him stride off into the night, confident, his back broad. Nothing she could do! Nothing she could do! Then who would help the forlorn girl? But wait — wait, she has promised nothing. Hero had forgotten too much; *she* had once slayed a dragon single-handedly in mortal combat. Hero's job was chronicling Sightings, who was to say her job wasn't the rescuing of forbidden princesses?

Amanda went back to the courtyard every night. She went at different times between control board duty, taking different alleys and streets, but she told no one because she was afraid they would forbid her — and Amanda had had enough pain from forbidden loves.

What would Mercie do in the city, with her powers confined by enchantment? she asked herself.

Each night when Amanda sat in the courtyard, she silently spoke the names of the King. Whenever the Forbidden Princess came to the balcony, Amanda closed her eyes, took sure aim, and with her powerful gift of seeing, pointed the names right at the girl's heart.

His Majesty ... my Sovereign Liege Lord ... His Eminence ... the Benevolent Potentate ... His Supreme Holiness ... the Lord Monsiegneur ... His Most Royal Highness ... the Monarch of All ... the true King ... to Him and to the Restoration of His Kingdom!

As Amanda did her lonely work, she watched for the slightest flicker of life in the eyes staring from the balcony, but there was nothing. Guilty memory taunted her — *forbidden love, forbidden love.* Crucial concentration came hard. Then one night as she sighted inwardly, she was sickened by seeing the evil eye of the Enchanter, searching, darting to and fro — and Amanda understood she was in peril. She knew she should end her vigils, but there — there! That very night, a tear dropped from the corner of the girl's eye. A sign of life! Amanda knew she had come again to love a thing dangerous to love.

So Amanda returned, hiding in the shadows of the cloisters, scarcely breathing lest she draw the ominous attention of the evil eye in the nearby Dagoda but aiming the Names from her heart to the heart of the girl standing on the balcony. At last, at last, the Forbidden

Princess lifted her eyes as though wakening from a trance, and then turned her head toward the shadows as though peering for the silent speaker of the Names.

The girl had been awakened. The Names had done their life-giving work. Now, how to get her out before horror overtook them both? A plan! Slip into the courtyard, hide; then help the princess escape in the daylight, when the city was sleeping.

Fit for a King

If impossible dreams are to come true, they require all the help we can get. If a task doesn't take much effort, it probably doesn't qualify as an impossible dream. What seemingly impossible dreams are you daring to dream?

Are you comfortable being around people who dream impossible dreams? I am. I enjoy hearing about grand schemes for making the world better. That's one reason Christ's kingdom, or kingship, message is so attractive to me. This world needs a righteous monarch who has both the wisdom to rule and the power to enforce His decisions. But it also needs someone marked by great love for all people. I believe Christ fills both those roles.

I'm happy to identify myself as one of His subjects, more than pleased to be involved in a small part of His marvelous now-and-future kingdom, and thrilled to tap into this incredible plan of His that gives such dignity and meaning and purpose to life. I also find there's enough room under His colossal umbrella to come up with challenging "impossible dreams" that are subpoints, or subdreams, of His.

When my dreams are consistent with Christ's dreams, I can expect His support in helping pull them off. The more my dreams overlap His, the more I can expect His aid when I need and request it.

Examine your dreams to see if there's a good reason to believe that the Lord will help you. Will God really benefit in any way if your dreams come true, or are the plans strictly of your own making and unrelated to what He's about?

Amanda's impossible dream was to rescue the Forbidden Princess from the hold of the Enchanter. Her glass-breaking idea was to see this sad young woman come to know the real King, and Amanda prayed for the princess, using his names. Would the King be of any help? Would he answer her prayers? Would he get involved in the rescue?

The next night Amanda left her earphones and headset hanging neatly on their hook, finished her dispatcher's notes, and crept without telling anyone into the little temple where she hid in the darkest corner. Finally, the gatekeeper turned the key in the outside lock. To her surprise she heard him say, *"She's locked inside."*

Which she? Amanda wondered. Her breath quickened. Eyes shut, looking inward, she was horrified to see the eye of the Enchanter looking straight at her! An evil smile lit up his face. Closing off sight, she hurriedly began the litany of names. This time, she spoke them aloud, urgently evoking the full sum of powers available to her.

"His Majesty the King!" The Forbidden Princess walked to the balcony. "My Sovereign Liege!" The girl leaned over the wrought iron, as Amanda herself walked boldly out of the shadows to the paving stones. "His Eminence!" The eyes of the Forbidden Princess filled with tears. "The Most Benevolent Potentate!" The tears splashed on the stones. "His Supreme Holiness!" The sky overhead began to shine slightly with a faint cast of dawn light. "The Lord Monsiegneur!"

The girl broke the silence and spoke, rather wept aloud hysterically, "It is too late—too late! Oh-oh-oh-oh! The Enchanter comes today to take me to the bridal chamber."

There was a pounding at the gate. BLAM! BLAM! BLAM! Amanda's heart failed. *Too late!* The distant echo of the death drums began to sound—*oom-bha-pah, oom-bha-pah*—calling sentries from the Dagoda to action.

What had she done? Awakened the princess out of her unfeeling numbness so she would be totally aware of the torture ahead? Placed her own valuable gifts of seeing and perfect aim as hostage to the enemy? These loves, these loves, these terrible loves! Would she never learn that love was dangerous? Why risk so much for one miserable girl among so many? Would she never learn about forbidden things?

The outer door—a key! Too late. The gatekeeper had returned.

Amanda drew herself to full stature and shouted the last names. "To the Monarch of All! To the King! To the Restoration of his Kingdom!" She knew she uttered treason and death was the penalty for her actions. But she was a princess of Great Park. Her heritage was of royal lineage; she would not whine or cry out or beg for mercy. For the sake of the King, she would march proudly to Burning Place.

Amanda held high her head as a man entered through the swinging gates.

He said, "Thank you, my sister. You honor me well." It was the King himself!

Amanda gasped. "But how? The locked latch—the key—" Through the open gates she could hear the death drums beating louder, faster.

"Did you forget that I can open all closed doors?"

He looked very plain. There were no golden highlights in his hair, his clothes were common—but the voice! It sounded of clear waters falling over great boulders, of winds blowing across fragrant fields. And the eyes! They contained the hush of the deep far sky itself, vast and infinite.

"Let us hurry to finish this work you have begun," he said, and he stepped beneath the balcony where the princess was weeping hysterically with her head hidden in her arms. "Beloved!" he called quietly. "My beloved!"

The girl raised her head, and her eyes grew wide and her weeping stopped. The voice of the One of the Names had spoken; she knew him instantly and reached out her hands in an appeal for rescue. Clambering up the vines to the balcony, the King quickly lowered the princess by her wrists to the courtyard stones.

"We are a little short of princesses right now where I come from," he explained gently after he himself had vaulted down. "They're all growing up and accomplishing great things in the world—"

When your impossible dream is obviously going to advance the kingdom, you have every reason to believe that the King will give your dream His full attention. This is true even if He doesn't demonstrate His support until what appears to be the last possible moment.

Dream Power

When considering the dreams or aspirations we hold, prayer becomes an important topic to be knowledgeable about. You see, dreams of any magnitude will burn you out if you substitute busyness for spiritual empowerment.

Obviously no one would knowingly make that mistake. But what happens is that the workload takes on a life of its own. The demands of the schedule gradually increase. The pressures become more and more immediate. God sometimes seems far away, so we take matters into our own hands.

After a while, prayer, which appears to have a slow payoff, seems to fight with the "more urgent matters," important things that just have to get done. We think *there's really nothing I can do to change that. Deadlines are deadlines.* Repeated days and weeks and months of pressure set us up in a pattern of racing around, and we think there's no longer enough time left for prayer. When that happens, the impossible dream becomes a monster, and must be pulled back on course.

That's what Jesus did in Mark 1:33-34: "The whole town gathered at the door, and Jesus healed many who had various diseases." Very early the next morning, while it was still dark, Jesus got up, left the house and went off to a solitary place, where He tried to get His schedule better organized.

That's not the way the passage reads, is it? That's what I would have done. But what Jesus did was to pray.

When Peter and his companions finally located Jesus they

said, "Everyone is looking for You!" (v. 37) (In other words: "Oh, You've been praying. How nice! Now let's get back to the crowd waiting for You. You won't believe how big it is!")

Somewhere along the line the apostles started to imitate their Lord. Acts 6 begins, "In those days when the number of disciples was increasing." What the Twelve did was to give over some of their responsibilities, their busyness, in order to "give [their] attention to prayer and the ministry of the word." Apparently the example of their Lord had had an impact on their thinking.

When we, like Jesus, empower our activities with prayer, God often sees to it that impossible dreams come true. And what great joy we experience just as the fictional Amanda felt when the King came to her aid.

He smiled at Amanda, the old, wonderful smile filled with kingslove, and for a moment it was as though they were in the Inner Circle surrounded by the dancing, leaping Sacred Flame. . . .

Relief flooded Amanda. She bowed her knee in a courtly curtsey and murmured, "My Liege Lord."

Then, sheltering the frightened girl in his arms, he said, "I think you had better come and be a princess in the company of my people."

In short order, they piled into a waiting taxi. To Amanda's surprise, Hero was sitting in the front seat. He reached over, gave her hand a squeeze and said, "Good work." How wonderful to be fellow to a brigade that could arrange last-minute rescues!

Amanda glanced through the open doors of the empty courtyard as the taxi pulled away. She felt relief, but — but jauntiness, too. Some of the old spirit of field and stream and childhood returned. A girl had been rescued from a terrible fate and was now nestled in the embrace of the King. No one — not Hero, not the cabbie, nor His Majesty — had scolded her with a "What-in-the name-of-Great-Park-possessed-you?"

She smiled back at Hero and was proud because *she* did not remind him that street wise, alley smart, he had said she could do nothing. It was true. She *had* done nothing. The Names and the King had done it all—but for a field child unused to city ways, she had done nothing very well indeed!

FOR DISCUSSION AND REFLECTION

1. What Hannah-like prayer requests have people shared with you that fit the impossible-dream category?

2. Do you personally hold on to any Hannah-like impossible dreams? If so, what are they?

3. How can you pray for these kinds of special requests in a way that it is to God's advantage to grant them?

4. What barriers keep you from praying in the way you would like?

5. Generally speaking, is your church stronger or weaker in the discipline of prayer than you are? Explain your answer.

6. What would you like to learn about prayer from someone stronger than you? What could you teach about prayer to someone less experienced than you are?

READINGS

If we are involved in the marketplace, we are trained to believe that time is money. That's why we talk about managing time, using it efficiently and profitably, and—as a result of our concern—dealing with time pressures.

Cram more in. Start earlier. Work later. Take work home. Dictate on the commuter train. Make phone calls in the car. Use a laptop computer in airports. Schedule breakfasts, lunches and dinners for profit. Performance, performance, performance—it's the key to promotion, to compensation increase, to power.

If an ordinary car engine turns four thousand revolutions per minute, a racing motor can turn up to ten thousand. The marketplace mentality says, "Rev that engine up to ten thousand as soon as you get up in the morning, and keep it there until you collapse in the sack at night."

Getting caught in that intense pace can be rewarding! It's exciting when the adrenaline starts to flow and you get on a roll, when your motor starts racing faster and faster. But it leaves precious little time for quiet moments with God.

You don't have to be in business to be overcommitted. Women with small children know what it means to do ten thousand RPMs all day long. Almost every minute of every minute of every day is consumed by those little creatures who pull on your pants legs, color on your walls, track mud on your carpet, throw food on your floor and then have the audacity to fuss in the middle of the night.

The pace of single, working parents is double or triple that of the rest of us. It is incomprehensible to me how they can meet the incessant demands of work all day and then go home to face the even more incessant demands of their children, with never any time out.

I see pastors, elders, church board members operating at the same relentless pace as everyone else. Never a dull moment; never a reflective moment either. Frightened, I ask myself, *Where does the still, small voice of God fit into our hectic lives? When do we allow Him to lead and guide and correct and affirm? And if this seldom or never happens, how can we lead truly authentic Christian lives?*

Too Busy Not to Pray, Bill Hybels, InterVarsity, pages 98–99.

■ ■ ■

In an era of anxiety and opportunities in which time is one of the most carefully guarded personal resources, why would people commit time to pray to a God with whom relatively few of them have a personal, life-defining relationship? Quite simply, Americans believe that prayer works. Americans are practical in using their resources. Those endeavors that demonstrate or maintain the promise of a good return on the investment of resources will continue to reap a commitment of those resources. Prayer, to date, meets the standard.

Almost 6 out of 10 adults (56%) say they are "absolutely certain" that prayer really makes a difference in their lives. An additional 1 out of 4 adults (23%) are "somewhat certain." Overall, this is 8 out of 10 people who remain at least partially persuaded that prayer has the power to affect their lives in a real way.

Interestingly, one out of five people who pray perceive prayer to be a gamble. They contend that they have no assurance or confidence in the power of prayer to make a difference, but they are hopeful it will work on their behalf.

"Look, it's a tough world out there. Does prayer really

work? How would I know? How would anybody know? It's a chance you take, but I figure it doesn't cost me anything and it can't hurt. It's kinda like playin' the lottery. You lose, you haven't lost much. You win, you hit the jackpot, and it's all worth it."

There may be reason to doubt whether many who pray are doing so with total confidence, but a surprisingly low proportion (just 11%) say they generally rely upon prayer as a last resort in difficult times. Rather, four out of five praying adults (82%) said that prayer is a regular part of their lives, regardless of the circumstances in which they find themselves.

Among the adults who pray to God, the frequency of their prayers is surprising. Almost 6 out of 10 (58%) claim that they pray every day. Just 1% state that they pray less than once a week; the rest of the respondents were distributed fairly evenly in terms of how many days a week they pray. Again, the types of people most likely to pray daily included women, nonwhites, churched people and Christians. Add to that senior citizens, people of lesser means and Protestants, and you have the segments most committed to regular prayer sessions. The types of people who stand out as the least likely to pray during the course of a week are residents of the Northeast and suburbanites.

When people pray, they usually pray more than once during the day. Among the people who pray, half (52%) say they usually pray more than once during the days they speak with God; 8% say that it varies, sometimes more than once, sometimes once; and about 4 out of 10 claim they typically pray once during those days they pray at all.

For most people, prayer is not a prolonged activity. The average amount of time adults spend in prayer is about 5 minutes. Overall, the study discovered that 1 out of 14 people (7%) who pray claim their average prayer time lasts between 15 and 30 minutes; another 6% stated that they usually prayed for more than 30 minutes each time they pray.

Absolute Confusion, George Barna, Regal, pages 95–96.

■ ■ ■

Too many of us have become so busy that we have little time for God. Our lives have become so busy that we have little time for God. Our lives have become obsessed with climbing the ladder of success and resting in the easy chair of entertainment. A prayerless church exists in this generation. We cannot get people to prayer meetings, but we have no problem amassing large crowds for Christian entertainment. Our church schedules are filled with events oriented toward entertainment, and we have no time left to seek God. We have become like the Laodicean church. Jesus is on the outside knocking, wanting to come in and have fellowship with us.

A.W. Tozer said, "For centuries the Church stood solidly against every form of worldly entertainment, recognizing it for what it was—a device for wasting time, a refuge from the disturbing voice of conscience, a scheme to divert attention from moral accountability. For this she got herself abused roundly by the sons of this world. But of late she has become tired of the abuse and has given over the struggle. She appears to have decided that if she cannot conquer the great god, Entertainment, she may as well join forces with him and make what use she can of his powers."

The Prayer Factor, Sammy Tippit, Moody, pages 50–51.

■ ■ ■

The men who have most fully illustrated Christ in their character, and have most powerfully affected the world for Him, have been men who spent so much time with God as to make it a notable feature of their lives. Charles Simeon devoted the hours from four till eight in the morning to God. Mr. Wesley spent two hours daily in prayer. He began at four in the morning. Of him, one who knew him well wrote: "He thought prayer to be more his business than anything else, and I have seen him come out of his closet with a serenity of face next to shining." John Fletcher stained the walls of his room by the breath of his prayers. Sometimes he would pray all night; always, frequently, and with great earnestness. His whole life was a life of prayer. "I would not rise from my seat," he said, "without lifting my heart to God." His greeting to a friend was always: "Do I meet you praying?" Luther said, "If I fail to spent two hours in prayer each morning, the devil gets the victory through the day. I have so much business I cannot get on without spending three hours daily in prayer." He had a motto: "He that has prayed well has studied well."

Preacher and Prayer, E.M. Bounds, Zondervan, page 38.

■ ■ ■

A PARABLE OF PRAYER

A father and his son, traveling together in a wagon,
  came to the edge of a forest.
Some bushes, thick with berries,
  caught the child's eye.
"Father," he asked, "may we stop a while
  so that I can pick some berries?"
The father was anxious to complete his journey,
  but he did not have it in his heart
  to refuse the boy's request.
The wagon was called to a halt,
  and the son alighted to pick the berries.

After a while,
  the father wanted to continue on his way.
But his son had become so engrossed in berry-picking
  that he could not bring himself to leave the forest.
"Son!" cried the father, "we cannot stay here all day!
  We must continue our journey!"

Even the father's pleas were not enough
  to lure the boy away.
What could the father do?
Surely he loved his son no less
  for acting so childishly.
He would not think of leaving him behind—
  but he really did have to get going on his journey.

Finally he called out:
  "You may pick your berries for a while longer,
  but be sure you are still able to find me.
  for I shall start moving slowly along the road,
As you work, call out 'Father! Father!'
  every few minutes, and I shall answer you.
As long as you can hear my voice,
  know that I am still nearby.
  But as soon as you can no longer hear my answer,
  know that you are lost,
  and run with all your strength to find me!"

Space for God, Don Postema, Bible Way, page 47.

CHAPTER SEVEN

MAKE GOD'S DREAMS FOR US OUR DREAMS AS WELL

A lot of people daydream about someday striking it rich. They fantasize how they'll spend their millions. Keeping that dream alive must be important, because some would-be millionaires actually gamble with their hard-earned money.

As an adult, for me the odds of winning a state lottery seem infinitesimally small. So I'm not tempted to save my money for a "glamorous fun-filled visit" to a gambling casino. I don't care if it's run by the Mafia or the government—count me out.

But back when I was in upper elementary school, a carnival came to our area in southern Illinois. The traveling company set up its wares in the big field at 30th and Main on the east edge of town. Our house was on 27th, just a couple of blocks away, so we neighborhood kids got to witness everything firsthand.

The giant Ferris wheel was the first attraction to go up. It was awesome. Then the tents and concession stands began to form a midway. Last, a huge net was hung on supports. It was designed to catch "Zaccheeni, the human cannonball." Each night he was shot from what looked like a cannon mounted on the back of a big flatbed truck. Because his flight path took him up over the Ferris wheel, I'm told almost everyone waited around to see what would happen.

The carnival officially opened on a Friday night, and I recall as a boy being in bed and hearing the music over the loud speakers. My folks said we could go during the day but not in the evening. So early the next morning I rendezvoused with friends, and we were off to see the wonders.

Step Right Up!

The tilt-a-whirl and the sword swallower and the shooting gallery caught the attention of my friends. But what I was fascinated by was a booth that featured what looked like miniature steam shovels. For a quarter a try you operated nobs that would make the claw (or the shovel) go up, down, and sideways, and open and close. Wonderful prizes were there to be picked up by this little shovel including, would you believe, a roll of five dollars worth of quarters. I watched a man win one of those rolls!

I saw others try and fail. But after a while I figured out what they were doing wrong. So eventually I just had to try my hand at it.

The test turned out to be harder than I had thought. And before I knew it, my only dollar was gone. However, on the last try I almost captured that elusive stack of quarters.

Now it was decision time. Back at home I had five dollars in my top dresser drawer. I was saving that to buy a new trick at Harry's Magic Shop. But with what I had already learned about the miniature steam shovels, I knew that in just another turn or two I could capture those quarters. Then I'd have my five dollars back, the dollar I had already lost, plus at least three or four dollars I wouldn't even have to spend.

I don't have to finish the story.

What was it that would prompt a boy to lose every cent he had on that stupid game? In the end I had absolutely nothing to show for my carnival experience—no hot dog, no pop, no ride on the octopus, nothing! I couldn't even tell my folks I'd had a great time.

Maybe it was the dream that I could get around the tough things all boys had to do to get "rich"—mow lawns, deliver papers, hawk ice cream at ball games. I don't know. But I do know that most days for most people are horribly routine, and life tends to go by rather quickly. All of that makes us susceptible to whatever appears a bit more exciting and bigger than life.

Tragic Decisions

There must have been a bit of a carnival atmosphere to traveling with Jesus. Certainly He drew great crowds. I wonder what the odds were that the Son of God would choose as one of His apostles a man who found money a bigger attraction than ministry. This member of the Twelve was supposedly laying up for himself treasures in heaven by being a part of Jesus' traveling entourage. But insiders testified that this disciple also worked at doing all right by himself here on earth as well!

Am I being too hard on Judas? I don't believe so.

Listen to these observations from his fellow apostle John. Remember the story in John 12 of Mary taking a pint of expensive perfume and pouring it on Jesus' feet? It was Judas who objected, asking, "Why wasn't this perfume sold and the money given to the poor?" (v. 5)

Here's John's contention (v. 6): "[Judas] did not say this because he cared about the poor but because he was a thief." That's a strong accusation, isn't it? Observe what John writes next: "As keeper of the money bag, [Judas] used to help himself to what was put into it." Wow!

I have to assume John is being truthful here. He reports that when Judas wanted to, he stole from the group's kitty. What this information reveals is that at the very least, for Judas the love of money was a strong enough urge that he was willing to steal.

We also know that for money—thirty pieces of silver—Judas was willing to turn informant.

Maybe that urge to be rich was there from the beginning. My suspicion is that initially Judas was captured by the person of Christ and His message about His kingdom, or kingship. Then when the miracles started happening and the crowds began to swell, Judas knew he was in on the ground floor of something unique. When a movement expands and experiences momentum like this, there's always the possibility of financial growth that can be exploited, which apparently is what Judas did.

But as months passed, and years, and the time eventually came for that final entry of the team into Jerusalem, Judas was quite aware that Jesus wasn't performing the way he felt He should. Christ wasn't taking advantage of "the messianic moment."

Realizing the kingdom wasn't going to be established the way he thought (i.e., a kingdom where he would have a prominent place), maybe this apostle felt he could best profit by disclosing the whereabouts of Christ to His enemies. Avarice would be a key motivation for Judas. That was, of course, a tragic decision.

When did the relationship between Judas and Jesus first begin to unravel? Was it back when Jesus said, "No one can serve two masters"? The two masters Christ named specifically were God and Money. We can't be sure when Judas first became disillusioned.

But in broad strokes, Judas' problem was that somewhere along the line his self-centered dreams took priority over Jesus' kingdom dream. How often that has happened with people who have followed Christ. Like Judas, they start thinking about money more than ministry.

Judas is an exception in the sense that he had the opportunity to spend so much time with Jesus. Certainly he should have figured out that in a relationship with Christ, when one gives priority to self-centered dreams it's not a win-win situation.

But Judas appears to be more the rule than the exception when we ask whether his attitude is a common one. The Jerusalem crowd had done the same thing earlier that week. They welcomed Christ into their city yelling, "Hosanna," a Hebrew expression meaning "save us now." Restated, "Deliver us from our oppressors and we'll buy into Your kingship, Jesus. We want You to be the promised Messiah. 'Blessed is He who comes in the name of the Lord!' "

Again here were self-centered dreams taking priority over what God had in mind for His Son to do. Therefore, this wouldn't have been a double win situation.

It's a win-win relationship when we learn to make God's dreams for us our dreams as well. Obviously it's a win for God because we are then His faithful servants. But it's also a win for us because we have a marvelous Lord who cares deeply about the well-being of His loyal subjects.

But we never want to forget that He is Lord and we are His servants. That's what Paul writes in 1 Corinthians 4:1-2.

"So then, men ought to regard us as servants of Christ and as those entrusted with the secret things of God. Now it is required that those who have been given a trust must prove faithful." Paul did this, but Judas did not.

One man started well and ended poorly. The other got off to a terrible start but eventually came on very strong. In God's kindness He didn't say to Paul that it was too late for him to buy into His kingship dream. The faithful servant is the one who takes great delight in the dreams of his master. And he or she is rewarded accordingly.

Throughout this book, I've been using sections from my wife, Karen's, and my Gold Medallion award-winning children's book, *Tales of the Resistance*.

Worth It All

In *Tales of the Resistance*, Big Operator, the head of the Resistance in Enchanted City, exemplifies the wonderful delight a subject takes in helping fulfill his King's dreams. Let me share a short section from the close of the story I used in chapter 4 called "The Orphan Exodus." Recall how the orphans responded to the King as he called each one by name.

Big Operator stood now at the street entrance to the pavilion; the beastly wolves lay silent in a stupor of sleep. He put two fingers to his mouth and blew a cabbie signal. At this, his master strategy went into operation. The first taxi accelerated to curbside, the first ready orphan group climbed into the back and front seats. The driver honked and then hurried off toward the garbage dump as another cab pulled up to take another load, followed by another and another.

And inside the King continued to speak the children's names, and with each naming the Orphan Keeper grew grayer, more haggard, leaking hot air. Her hair lost its luster, her teeth grew black and straggly until all could see her for her true self: a wicked hag who had gorged on the energy and youth and beauty of the children given to her keeping, a faker whose evil power was not her own, a no-people in disguise, as were all who gave themselves to do the will of the Enchanter. Finally she was nothing but a pile of dust covered by filthy red and purple rags, her gold melted and her jewels turned to powder.

And Big Operator was glad; his heart leaped with gladness. He knew the Enchanter would take revenge, but if this be his last strategic rescue design ever, he had been at the side of his King as together they emptied the pavilion of every last orphan. He closed his eyes and listened to the taxi vanguard, *his* taxi vanguard, honking throughout all of Enchanted City. HARNK! HARNK!—here, there, and everywhere—HARNK! HARNK! It sounded in his ears like a raucous chorus of jubilant rescue.

The King stood beside him ready to leave and to accompany the escapees into Great Park. The handclasp between them was firm and long. Their anger was gone but, strangely, there was no exultation, just a quiet sadness. Both knew what dire consequences their defiant acts would set into motion. "Farewell," said the King, and they embraced, the embrace of two mighty men. The orphan exodus was accomplished.

Big Operator watched the King disappear into the night. And though he knew it was just his imagination, it seemed as though a crowd of children stood all over the city, clapping their hands and shouting "Bravo!" And when the last taxi had hurried away with the last load, on a whim Big Operator bowed to the city—and the applause rose louder in his heart.

For Big Operator had learned through the years of masterminding the taxi resistance that mighty deeds demand mighty risks, but that it is worth risking all for the sake of the Kingdom and the King.

It's worth the risk!

To think this way is not easy. But all things being equal, making Christ your Ruler results in the best life you can have in this world! How's that for a glass-shattering idea?

So be careful what you make your ultimate dream. Don't end up snookered and broke and embarrassed. Remember that Christ has all eternity to reward you for whatever suffering you receive on His behalf.

The Restoration Is Near!

Here's another short section from *Tales of the Resistance*. The evil Enchanter has taken his awful revenge on Big Operator and his taxi resistance. He's trying to find the young King and destroy him as well. This is a conversation between two resistance members, young Hero and Amanda.

Hero sighed. The Chronicle was almost current. The orphan exodus had been recorded and he had only to write about these recent terrible events. "I think I can remember everything Big Operator ever said to me." He leaned back in the chair and quoted the chief. " 'This is an occupied city; we are in the midst of enemy territory.'

"He was a rough man, Amanda, — but, everyone in the City Taxi Company knew he was a man of the mind as well. It was the chief who collected the fragments of song and unwritten stories from the tale keepers for the Chronicle. Without them that history would be almost forgotten — the tales of the always young King who once ruled this city with a firm but benevolent hand, of the Age of Rebellion when the Enchanter lured away the loyalty of the citizenry, of how the King went into exile vowing to return when time enough had passed for all to discover the folly of such a choice, and of how the fire wizard placed an enchantment over the city and ruled his subjects with the power of fire."

Hero paused, remembering. "My own mother must have been a tale keeper — keeping alive the old, true tales. I remember her words on her dying bed: 'There is a King, a real King!' "

Amanda felt tired and saddened. When would they ever be able to go back to the old ways of field and forest?

"You love him, don't you?" she said, smiling gently.

"Yes," said Hero. "He's a gruff old gizzard, but he's a genius, too. He'd been experimenting with daylight. 'The whole city's supposed to run on it!' he'd say. Solar panels. Storage cells. Sun batteries. He was getting us ready to live in the Restoration, to live at day and sleep at night, to harness the sun to do the work that slave labor does now."

Amanda quoted Big Operator: "Work in harmony with the world; not in disharmony with it!" She punched the air with her fist. This was a favorite City Taxi Company saying; they almost heard his rough voice again. The two smiled sadly at each other.

With that Hero leaned his elbows forward on the desk and hid his face in his hands. His voice was tight with grief. "He's dead, Amanda. I know it in my heart. I can only hope that he died quickly."

The two were silent. Amanda didn't protest, didn't work to evoke false hope. She had already seen this terrible truth deep in her own heart. After a while she spoke, "Did anyone tell you what Big Operator's last words were when he was taken captive? You'll need it for the Chronicle."

Hero shook his bowed head, and she continued. "He had been badly beaten; three or four Breakers attacked him. Destruction was dismantling his lifework; but as they were dragging him away, he struggled to his feet and called out for all of us to hear above the din, 'The Restoration is near!' They knocked him senseless as he must have known they would. But, Hero, I keep hearing his cry, over and over—'The Restoration is near!'"

"The restoration is near"—believe me, that's a great truth to live by. Yes, our King's dream will know fulfillment.

Personal dreams related only to this life are never enough. They will always come up short. They don't span time and eternity. That's why, even as Christians, when we give priority to self-centered dreams, we lose.

Don't view Jesus' role in your life primarily as someone to help you get what you have in mind—be it wealth, health, a comfortable life, security, a ripe old age, recognition, or power. That approach is precarious at best. It's the path Judas followed. It's the servant thinking about the master, "I look at you as a means for me to reach the goals on *my* agenda." That's the reverse of the way it should be. Good servants don't think or act in that manner.

What does a trustworthy servant keep as foremost in his or her mind? The desires and dreams of the master.

In that context the good Master, the gracious Lord, the true King of the universe, will see to it that such a servant is treated better than the best. Again, it's a win-win relationship when we learn to make God's dreams for us our dreams as well.

Now there's a good gamble. I can almost hear the other eleven apostles saying, "Amen! Amen!"

FOR DISCUSSION AND REFLECTION

1. Think about someone you know who once walked close to the Lord but no longer does. Without naming the person, tell what you think happened.

2. Which is more likely—gradually drifting away from the Lord or turning away from Him suddenly? Why?

3. Explain how a church that was once close to the Lord could begin giving priority to more self-centered dreams.

4. How closely do your personal dreams align with what you feel God would say His dreams are for you?

5. Share a personal "Big Operator event," a time of great satisfaction when you felt you brought your King great pleasure.

6. Give specific reasons why it is a win-win relationship when we make God's dreams for us our dreams as well.

READINGS

After two years of college and the study of business theory nearly bored me to death, I returned to the family business prepared to follow in my father's footsteps. I loved the adrenaline of the marketplace. I was charged by the challenge — to do things a little more efficiently, to organize better, to maximize resources. And to make a ton of money. I knew where I was headed and what I wanted.

And then came a leading from the Holy Spirit. The director of a Christian camp I worked at during the summers pulled me off to the side and asked me a question that shook me to my foundations. "Bill, what are you doing with your life that will last forever?" The question haunted me. I began to realize that my whole existence was wrapped around the here and now. Everything I was doing was self-centered and temporary. That question stripped me naked, and I discovered that without the planes and boats and fast cars I had little to give my life meaning. As I continued to work at the produce company, I felt more and more restless. Finally, I decided I needed to serve the Lord more directly. I wanted to be on the front lines of the spiritual battle.

When I told my dad of my decision, he said, "Fine, Bill. Now turn in your credit cards and your keys to the plane, the boat, and the cars. And don't entertain any ideas of coming back."

I got a job in a shipping department of a Christian organization in the Chicagoland area. I made minimum wage. I was nineteen. I'll never forget the time my father flew in to visit me. I was standing between two middle-aged women, stuffing little plastic awards into cellophane wrappers. My dad looked at his son, for whom he had held such high hopes. Not one usually given to changing his mind, he took me to lunch and said, "You can get on that plane with me and come home." I told him no; I didn't want to miss the adventure. And I meant it!

Descending into Greatness, Bill Hybels and Rob Wilkins, Zondervan, pages 206–7.

■ ■ ■

Not many months after my conversion, having a leisure afternoon, I retired to my own chamber to spend it largely in communion with God. Well do I remember that occasion. How in the gladness of my heart I poured out my soul before God; and again and again confessing my grateful love to Him who had done everything for me — who had saved me when I had given up all hope and even desire for salvation — I besought Him to give me some work to do for Him, as an outlet for love and gratitude; some self-denying service, no matter what it might be, however trying or however trivial; something with which He would be pleased, and that I might do for Him who had done so much for me. Well do I remember, as in unreserved consecration I put myself, my life, my friends, my all, upon the altar, the deep solemnity that came over my soul with the assurance that my offering was accepted. The presence of God became unutterably real and blessed; and though but a child under sixteen, I remember stretching myself on the ground, and lying there silent before Him with unspeakable awe and unspeakable joy.

For what service I was accepted I knew not; but a deep consciousness that I was no longer my own took possession of me, which has never been effaced. It has been a very practical consciousness. Two or three years later propositions of an unusually favorable nature were made to me with regard to medical study, on the condition of my becoming apprenticed to the medical man who was my friend and teacher. But I felt I dared not accept any binding engagement such as was suggested. I was not my own to give myself away; for I knew not when or how He whose alone I was, and for whose disposal I felt I must ever keep myself free, might call for service.

Within a few months of this time of consecration the impression was wrought into my soul that it was in China the Lord wanted me. It seemed to me highly probable that the work to which I was thus called might cost my life; for China was not then open as it is now. But few missionary societies had at that time workers in China, and but few books on the subject of China missions were accessible to me. I learned, however, that the Congregational minister of my native town possessed a copy of Medhurst's *China,* and I called upon him to ask a loan of the book. This he kindly granted, asking me why I wished to read it. I told him that God had called me to spend my life in missionary service in that land. "And how do you propose to go there?" he inquired. I answered that I did not at all know; that it seemed to me probable that I should need to do as the Twelve and the Seventy had done in Judea—go without purse, or scrip, relying on Him who had called me to supply all my need. Kindly placing his hand upon my shoulder, the minister replied, "Ah, my boy, as you grow older you will get wiser than that. Such an idea would do very well in the days when Christ Himself was on earth, but not now."

I have grown older since then, but not wiser. I am more than ever convinced that if we were to take the directions of our Master and the assurances He gave to His first disciples more fully as our guide, we should find them to be just as suited to our times as to those in which they were originally given.

To China with Love, J. Hudson Taylor, Dimension, pages 14–16.

■ ■ ■

"He is no fool who gives what he cannot keep to gain what he cannot lose." *(1949)*

"One treasure, a single eye, and a sole master." *(1948)*

"God, I pray Thee, light these idle sticks of my life and may I burn for Thee. Consume my life, my God, for it is Thine. I seek not a long life, but a full one, like you, Lord Jesus." *(1948)*

"Father, take my life, yea, my blood if Thou wilt, and consume it with Thine enveloping fire. I would not save it, for it is not mine to save. Have it Lord, have it all. Pour out my life as an oblation for the world. Blood is only of value as it flows before Thine altar." *(1948)*

"Saturate me with the oil of the Spirit that I may be aflame. But flame is often short-lived. Canst thou bear this, my soul? Short life? In me there dwells the spirit of the Great Short-Lived, whose zeal for God's house consumed Him. 'Make me Thy fuel, Flame of God.' " *(1948)*

Shadow of the Almighty, Elisabeth Elliot, Harper and Brothers, page 247.

■ ■ ■

What difference do you make to those who love you and serve you with enthusiasm? You allow them the indescribable joy of contemplating you.

You have given me a special insight into the sweetness of your love: you gave me my life; when I wanted far away, you brought me back again to serve you; you wanted me to love you.

You are a waterfall of unceasing love! What shall I say about you? How can I forget you? You thought of me even when I was lost and desperate. You have been merciful beyond my wildest dream. You have been good to me far above anything I deserve.

How shall I pay you back? Most of us are not expected to give up everything, to renounce the world and begin a life of monastic solitude. Does it mean very much that I should serve you when all of creation exists for that purpose? I don't think so. But I see this, and it staggers me: you are willing to accept the service of someone as poor and unworthy as I. You will make me one of your beloved servants.

I am your servant! Everything I have is yours. But even as I say that, I know you are serving me more than I am serving you. At your command all of the resources of heaven and earth are at my disposal, and even the angels help me. Yet you serve me in a way that surpasses all of this: you promise to give yourself to me. You are the great Servant of us all.

With what gift can I return your favors? I want to serve you all the days of my life. I wish it were possible, just for one day, to do something worthwhile for you. You are my Lord, and I am a poor servant who is obligated to serve you with all my strength. I should never tire of praising you, for this is what I want to do. This is my desire. Compensate for what I lack.

The Imitation of Christ, Thomas à Kempis, Harold Shaw, pages 115–16.

■ ■ ■

The connection between faith and deeds, between spirituality and compassion, has societal dimensions, not just personal ones. The great philosopher of religion Elton Trueblood noted the role of religious faith in society when he wrote, "The terrible danger of our time consists in the fact that ours is a *cut-flower civilization.* Beautiful as cut flowers may be, and much as we may use our ingenuity to keep them looking fresh for a while, they will eventually die, and they die because they are severed from their sustaining roots. We are trying to maintain the dignity of the individual apart from the deep faith that every man is made in God's image and is therefore precious in God's eyes." We believe the saints among us are in touch with a transcendent dimension that more than many people realize, may be the hope of civilization.

Nancy Longhurst, a young woman in her twenties, is one saint who shows this connection through a simple but significant story. She was in church one morning when a couple who worked with children with disabilities and profound retardation stood to talk about their work. "I remember clearly sitting in the church," she says, "and feeling strongly that that is what I should do, even though I had never done it before and was a bit afraid of people with disabilities." Living largely off savings, she spent the next year in the couple's household. Through being with them and watching how they treated the children they cared for, she says, "seeing how their philosophy was always to approach a child with love, I learned to care for people. I learned that that has to be at the heart of this field: to serve people as Christ would serve."

Historian Glenn Tinder has put Nancy's discovery in more academic terms to suggest something similar. Ultimately, he argues, "good customs and habits need spiritual grounds, and if those are lacking, they will gradually, or perhaps suddenly in some crisis, crumble." We cannot think that there are no societal implications from the secularization our culture has experienced in recent decades, he believes. We wrongly assume that we can continue to treasure "the life and welfare, the civil rights and political authority, of every person without believing in a God who renders such attitudes and conduct compelling." Tinder asks, "To what extent are we now living on moral savings accumulated over many centuries but no longer being replenished? To what extent are those savings already severely depleted?"

If the dominant message we get from the culture is that *our* needs, *our* ambitions, *our* self-fashioned goals for life are all that matters, we need the saints among us to remind us differently. While we are told that we have a right to live for ourselves, buy what satisfies our whims, and think little about God or others, the saints model something else. By their convictions and by their behavior they can remind us how to live, and where to find the resources to act on our higher impulses, as a society and as members of society.

The Saints Among Us, George H. Gallup, Jr. and Timothy Jones, Morehouse, pages 73–74.

CHAPTER EIGHT

THINK PROACTIVELY INSTEAD OF REACTIVELY

It was not long ago that two young men, Bill Clinton and Al Gore, were voted into the top leadership positions of our United States government. They were the first of the Baby Boomers to become President and Vice-President.

Some viewed them as youthful, inexperienced, and even dangerous. Others said change was needed, and these men were at least talking about the right kinds of dreams. Those voters agreed with the media, that President Bush couldn't articulate a vision. The incumbent was obviously frustrated by the accusation. What was wrong with "traditional family values"? That approach had worked well in 1988. But somewhere along the way those words apparently had lost their magic, and now they sounded outdated, right of center, and too narrow for many 1992 voters.

Maybe it was just one of those times when change was inevitable. On the world scene communism had collapsed. And the U.S. military had convinced everyone of its overwhelming superiority in the *miracle-fast* Gulf War.

So to many at home, it seemed like a good opportunity to try fresh approaches—approaches that would benefit more than just the so-called establishment. Now was the time, during this new period of peace, to reduce our spending, to favor the working people instead of the wealthy, and to look at global concerns such as ecology and world hunger.

Today the nation is seeing change, that's for sure! Some of it is good; some is scary. But it's certainly true that these men are taking us down new paths.

The Ultimate Visionary

Maybe my comments on U.S. politics will help you appreciate some of what was experienced by segments of the Jewish population in Jesus' day. Of course, He was significantly younger than either of our present leaders. Jesus was only in His early thirties when He started campaigning for a change in leadership.

Jesus' visionary presentation—His dream—was about a new kind of kingdom, or kingship. Christ was saying that for people to know a better world, they needed to willingly recognize Him as their rightful leader, or king. Wherever He went He talked about this kingship, or kingdom. In a most appealing manner, He said that it was to the advantage of His hearers to buy into what He was offering.

"The leaders you have now—when you're in deep sorrow, when you mourn, do they comfort you? Is that what Herod does? No. But you're blessed, *my* friends, because now you can come under *my* rule. Under *my* kingship, those who mourn are comforted. Watch how I live among you. My way of life verifies what I'm telling you."

"Listen to Me, this is good news! Do you hunger and thirst for righteousness, for what's right in the eyes of God? In Pilate's hall of judgment, is that where you expect to find righteousness? You know better. But under *My* kingship, you'll discover what you're looking for. I'll show you what's right in God's eyes. When I'm on the throne, you'll be satisfied and blessed.

"You who are meek—yes, you, and you, ma'am—is it to your advantage to be meek under Caesar? Not really. But under *My* reign it's the meek—yes, you—who will inherit the earth."

Christ's kingdom talk was electrifying! The Jewish population longed for the revealing of the anointed one of God, the great Jewish King who had been promised, their Messiah. That's what the word *Messiah* means, "the anointed of God." The word *Christ* means the same thing. It's Greek for "the anointed one." *Christ* and *Messiah* are synonyms. One is a Greek word, the other is Hebrew. If I say Jesus Christ, that means the same as Jesus Messiah, Jesus the anointed one.

Anti-Establishment

For some years the little country of Israel had been buzzing with Messiah talk. Stories had been circulating for twenty to thirty years about a miracle child King Herod had tried to kill, but who had escaped unharmed.

This kind of Messiah talk always made the Roman forces edgy, even with their overwhelming military superiority.

I'm sure the Jewish leadership of the time saw this newcomer Jesus as youthful. They probably did not appreciate His criticism of their traditional values. In fact, over the months and years, the young Jesus became increasingly dangerous in the minds of the establishment.

But they couldn't articulate an alternative vision that captured the fancy of the people. Yes, they had a power, of sorts, but there was no longer any magic in their words. They knew they were no match for Christ, especially when He demonstrated supernatural powers.

For the Sanhedrin to affirm His message would require changes few in their ranks were willing to make. Here was a glass ceiling they had no intention of breaking. Their bottom line, wealth, seemed to have little meaning to Jesus. What mattered to Him was love—love for God and love for others. Treating people the way you wanted them to treat you was what He advocated.

In a way, Jesus was a bit of a comic figure to the leaders of His day. He seemed so naive, so idealistic, so ignorant of politics and power. "Treat others the way you want them to treat you." Anybody with the least amount of sense could figure out in an instant how to take advantage of that philosophy. This was especially true of the Romans.

There are eras when nothing changes, no matter what. Then there are times when change is in the air. You can sense it coming; it appears inevitable. This was one of those times.

What would happen? Obviously the Jewish religious system wasn't working well, except for the pious few.

Good or bad, it wasn't long before the Jewish Council members knew that Jesus was walking a different path than they were. By Passover of His final year, it looked as if the crowds were following Him. They were crying, "Hosanna! Blessed is He who comes in the name of the Lord!"

Even a few months back, who would have thought this possible? It made the religious right nervous. They would have to do all they could to defeat Him before the ground-swell became too great to stop.

This is not an appropriate place for me to express my feelings about President Clinton and Vice-President Gore. But I don't hesitate to tell you that I really like this King Jesus I see in the Scriptures. He was one of a kind! For someone in His early thirties, He showed *remarkable* maturity.

Unfortunately, it's hard to describe Jesus in fresh terms. So much has been written about Him. These words from *Tales of the Resistance* describe a fictional king. They might give us a fitting picture of King Jesus as well.

Thespia had fallen hopelessly in love with the King. Oh, not the actor/king (though he was handsome and her ardent admirer), but the mythical king of the play—the one who was strong but not brutal, who could laugh with joy and weep with freedom, who never leered at beautiful women, who told stories to children and gentled the fears of the old, whom the young men followed because he was the bravest of all, who found beauty in the ugly, and whose very words spoke hope.

Like Thespia, I too love this young King. I like the man, and I like His plan—His dream for the world.

I believe that if we all lived as He did, if we all said, "Jesus, Your thoughts will be my thoughts. Your ways, Jesus, will be my ways. Your rule, Jesus, the rule I swear allegiance to above all else"—this sad world would become a most wonderful place almost overnight. We would know the joy of having food for all, dignity for all, peace over all. In fact, I don't think there's any other way to make the world work. I really don't!

You love this King too, don't you?!

The Best Died Young

The world shouldn't kill its good men and women. Dreamers are too rare to begin with. But sometimes the world destroys its best.

Jimmy Carter was a national leader and a man of noble dreams. He still is. If we heard that authorities somewhere had arrested him and beaten him in Rodney King fashion, and in the process of carrying out supposed justice they had killed him, we would be shocked. "What has the world come to?" we would ask.

When Gallup polls ask who are the most admired men and women, what names are predictable?

* Billy Graham
* The pope
* Mother Teresa
* President Clinton
* Colin Powell
* Barbara Bush

Let them all live to old age. Don't kill the good ones off.

Thank goodness there were no headlines twenty or thirty years ago declaring "Billy Graham Shot And Killed While Sharing God's Good News"!

When attempts of deranged individuals or hired assassins fail and the pope lives or President Reagan is only wounded, I thank the Lord.

Yet how can it be that in the long history of the world the finest of all persons would be arrested as a young man and roughed up and tried and spit on and convicted of blasphemy by the Jewish high court? That both Herod and Pilate would remove themselves from the process of justice and say to a hired crowd, "I've whipped Him senseless. Isn't that enough for you? All right, then, what you do to Him next is your responsibility, not mine."

Have I gotten past your mind to your feelings yet? That's what I've been attempting to do.

Fiction has a way of putting us in touch with our emotions and giving us new insights. Like C.S. Lewis in *The Lion, the Witch and the Wardrobe,* a fiction writer says in essence, "Let me take you to another world. If you can see what's happening there, maybe you can better comprehend what takes place in your own world." Let's return to Enchanted City, where another young woman who loves the King, Amanda, has sneaked into the court to observe his trial. All seems discouraging and unfair and hopeless and heavy.

"First witness," cried the Clerk.

It was the Chief Herald, the one formerly known as Doublespeak. His friends said that he was Doublespeak no more, but Doomster, the one who pronounced judgment for the Enchanter. The emblem of the fire wizard was emblazoned on his elegant purple jersey; he wore brass armbands and a circlet of gold upon his head. "Why, I heard, I heard with my very own ears this man, this prisoner there, proclaim another kingdom, where the subjects live in the light. He attempted to entice me, me, the Chief Herald to the Enchanter, to treason."

Someone in the courtroom called out, "Treachery!" Another shouted, "Death to pretenders!"

The Clerk banged his gavel for order. The man in the center of the courtroom spoke not a word.

Amanda studied him carefully. His shoulders sagged as though he was suffering great sorrow. He seemed drawn within himself—the proceedings in that place made no difference. It was as though he had walked into a great aloneness and was not even present.

Seeing! thought Amanda. If she could see into the King's mind. Closing her eyes, Amanda aimed her gifts at the great soul of the man standing in disguise before her. A wave of enormous sadness overcame her. Tears began to stream down her cheeks and she was tempted to withdraw her sight. *"Nay-nay-nay,"* intoned the song of doom. The King's mind was entering into every dark place in Enchanted City—no, more—taking all the darkness into his very center.

Amanda could see nothing. The dark blindness overwhelmed her, but somehow she realized that her sight labored by the side of her dear King, the one she loved most in all the world.

"My Liege Lord," she whispered in her heart, and the man in front of her stirred slightly, as though he had heard and recognized her words with his own soul. It was then Amanda realized that nothing could be done, that for now, there was no light in the King, that he had for some reason of his own knowing joined with this deepest and most impenetrable darkness.

Through him Amanda stared into the shadow of death itself, into the night of all nights that begins and has no ending, and she withdrew, opening her eyes, unable to bear any more the grimacing features of total despair.

It was then she saw them, circling the rim of the court-yard, standing beyond and above and over the Burners and Breakers: gorgeous, brilliant, shining—the Bright Ones! They were translucent, shimmering. As Amanda glanced quickly at the miserable creatures sitting on benches, cold, shivering with fear, hopeless, glad for one wretched moment of reprieve at the expense of the most beautiful man who ever lived, the princess realized that no one else was aware of these creatures of indescribable glory.

Unknowing, they were all surrounded by these exquisite, unseen beings who glistened like raindrops on cobwebs blown by the wind, who turned like gossamer milkpod seeds in the brilliant sunlight, who raised their eyes filled with star glory, and stretched their wings, tip to tip, now gold, now silver, now pure light on light. The Bright Ones bent their graces toward the man in the center of this trial, preventing any interruption of purpose from breaking his intense concentration.

Their looks focused on the King in the center, holding off tenderness, staying any loving-kindness lest goodness distract him from the work of breaking the Enchanter's spell, which held all the city in its grip. They were not helping him; they were only keeping him from being interrupted. Amanda could see that they, too, wept.

The Princess turned her moist and opened eyes to the King. Now she understood that he was deliberately restraining his own power. He was not defeated by the gathering evil oppression in this hold of the fire wizard.

The King was holding himself in, containing command and nobility, silencing his majestic authority, confining his royalty in order to descend by the way of mind and spirit into the center of dark agony, the very secret evil crux of the Enchanter's domain. He was preparing *himself* to be the willing victim who would lift the enchantment from the city.

It was then Amanda realized that the trial had gone on, that other witnesses had been called, that now the courtroom was a chaos of noise. "Burn him! Burn him!" the people screamed. "Death to the pretender!" pronounced the Chief Herald.

"TO THE BURNING PLACE!" screamed the Enchanter, and the iron cauldrons flared orange at the pronouncement of sentence. The death drums rolled. The pokers of the Burners glowed. The fire wizard removed his black robe of condemnation. The gavel pounded, raising sparks.

Amanda's heart broke at this judgment and she sobbed aloud, no longer hiding herself. For once it made no matter, for the evil eye sought only one victim, one sacrificial captive, and that One remained still, silent in the rising riot as the Enchanter began for procession of death.

So the Enchanter's men came a last time and took into custody the One who could walk into the center of madness, who could make his way into the underworld of each child's life, whose very name freed the prisoner, whose promise of a Kingdom made life worth playing, who brought light into all dark places. The One who could sing the whole song, who could call each orphan by name. The only One who could stare the Enchanter in the eye, who could challenge the very dominion of evil. The One who begins the dance of celebration again at life's end—the King, the true King.

When someone you deeply love is suddenly killed, it leaves you stunned.

When that death is a violent one, and the person's body is mutilated, you feel even worse.

When torture is involved, friends feel violated themselves, physically sick, deeply disturbed, confused.

* "I just saw him alive and well, smiling and waving to the crowds. It was on TV—he was in a convertible driving through downtown Dallas. Jackie was there by his side. Then there were these shots from somewhere. Apparently a couple of bullets just tore his head open."

* "World leaders waving to the crowds—where was it? The Summit in Vancouver, or the Passover celebration in Jerusalem? When was that? Just last week, wasn't it? Yes, he smiled and waved, beautiful smile. Now he's dead?"

* "He must have been the most wonderful leader the world has ever known, the person who had the most amazing ideas, the most thrilling of dreams. It's a tragedy—what a loss. Who could possibly ever replace him?"

A torch is lit. The priest touches it to the pyre. The flames burst into the night. They whoosh; they burn; they leap higher and higher. The wild wind roars, feeding the conflagration. The shadow at the stake lifts, arches, raises its head, and is crowned with burning.

The Enchanter is a writhing, frenzied silhouette before the fire. He lifts his distorted face to the flames, "Owa-ha-ha! Owa-ha-ha!—the howl of a beast over its prey. OWA-HA-HA! OWA-HA-HA!

But each common man stands pierced to the soul, watching the crackling flames, the leaping cinders, the chorus of fire singing raucously upon the pyre. For all know now, though they may forget it tomorrow: the wizard will feel joy at any burning place, at any death time, at any agony of final passing. He will preside in gleeful dance at any dying. . . .

In the darkness, a crowd begins to gather, a throng, all those who have loved and served the King, all those who have worked in the resistance; each man, woman, and child who ever dared to believe in the breaking of enchantments or dared to hope in a future restoration. All who longed for the exile to end now stand mourning in the ashes of the death of all dreams and try to re-member light, and song, and life. . . .

A beautiful woman with flaxen hair falls to her knees in the ash dust. Will she never again act out stories in the streets? ... Will she nevermore speak the rhymes of peace, the poetry of hope, the prose of power? Will the memory of the tale be broken, the most wonderful story of all be locked away in the archives, never to be retold?

The Keeper of the Chronicle of Sightings of the King stands silent, too, stripped of hope, ravaged. The Enchanter is the victor after all, death his second-in-command. *There is no such thing as a Kingdom,* he thinks. *Great Park is only make-believe. ...I am no Hero, nor a King's man. The city saying is so: "There is no such thing as a King." This is and will ever be the keep of the Great Enchanter.*

He holds the handle of the hatchet by his side, feeling no power. *We have tricked ourselves,* he thinks and casts the tool to the ground. Then he sits in the ashes, his heart too much of stone for weeping.

He stares at the gathering crowd, shadows in the blackness. *Why are they here? It's all over. We all are orphans, all ugly deformed scarboys, sewer rats and boiler brats, carnival girls, heralds of untruths.* And we must all return to Enchanted City, this place of the no-people. The time for heroics is ended.

He sits motionless; he sleeps but sees no visions. Numb, he rests not. He wakes to darkness; no day comes. Will this night never end? All is done. Over. Never to be again, a forever unhappiness.

In the night, he thinks that the shadows, forms deeper than the substance of darkness, creep closer to the pyre which rises black, a rubble of twisted cinder and charcoal, in the middle of Burning Place. Someone stands beside him, and reaches to him a hand. It is an old, old woman, more bent than ever, the grasp now feeble. It is Mercie.

"Why are they here?" he asks her, motioning to the shadows. "Must all who love him come?"

Her voice is weak; her answer sounds far away. "Yes. All who love the King must come to this place before they can see the Restoration begin."

He wants to scoff. He wants to shout silence, but his eye is caught by a tiny glow on the pyre—*embers that are not completely burned.* Others in the gathered congregation of shadows see it, too; they gasp. Peering, he rises to his knees, but wait! The glow suddenly becomes a flame, one small warm ring of light, not an angry destroying rage, but a good burning, a flower flame, growing strangely larger and larger, unfolding upon itself, petals of soft fire, layer upon layer opening outward, white, rose, golden, glowing.

In this sudden light, he can see that the shadows are the people of Great Park who have stood in the darkness, waiting, waiting. Here a band of Rangers in forest garb. There orphans newly arrived, their faces scrubbed but filled with anxiety. He spies Amanda. This has been a night of anguish for her; her face is haggard, but her eyes—they seem to be filled with sight. And beyond them all, strange forms of soft, almost indistinguishable luminescence.

As the flower of fire grows, he sees his comrades from the taxi resistance, people of the city, brave men and women whose faces are now filling with wonder. Nearby stands Caretaker, his back straightening in the warmth of the new flame.

Then out of the center of the lovely burning light, a laugh! His heart leaps. He has heard that laugh before. His being lurches with hope.

It is the laugh of the King!

All stare into the middle of the death field, into the flaming flower, their mouths agape, their eyes open wide. A form is taking shape in the middle of the pistils and the stamen. A real form is rising from the burning center. It gathers unto itself, becoming distinct, definite, firm. The watchers narrow their vision in order to see better what they can scarcely believe they are seeing. It's the King—the King! He stands tall, stands bold. He stamps a foot—sending flames dancing into the night. He lifts his arms in exultation. He throws back his head and laughs—the Challenger, the conqueror laughs the first laugh of creation again and again and again.

Suddenly, in the middle of that blackest night, right at midnight, when stars, moons, and planets are utterly dimmed by enchantment, day comes. Light splits the darkness again. Day falls upon Enchanted City—shafts of glorious light, brilliant rays of brightness, dawning come untimely. And the King in the center of the burning field lifts his face to the warm new sun and at that, the flowering fire quiets and the King steps from the flames.

And all see at once that he is the meaning of the dance; he is the other side of the death place, his word weaves universe out of chaos; he is the restorer of all lost cities; his life is the potion all must take against enchantment.

The great crowd of subjects of the King ring Burning Place. A circle, a great vast circle, stretches around the dusty rim of the death field. They join hands, reaching to their neighbor, young to old, woman to man, adult to child. From the center of the burning flower, quieted but still luxuriant with light, the familiar music begins. It is the music of the Great Celebration. *Ah-h-h-h-h,* they have heard this before; *ah-h-h-h-h,* slowly, very slowly, the great circle begins to turn.

Hero watches the graceful movements. But the people are not changed. Is becoming over? *Will we never be real again,* he wonders, *become who we really are?*

"Hero!" a Ranger friend calls. "Are you no longer dancing?"

The music quickens as the King in the center stoops and lifts an armful of flame which shimmers and flutters in his embrace, alive. And as the dance passes, he tosses a flower to this one, to that until the whole moving ring is filled with brilliant light, like comets, like galaxies of orbiting moons. And Hero watches as each now becomes, not passing through the Circle of Sacred Flames, but being passed through themselves by holy light as the shining fires disappear only to shine brightly from each one's eyes.

Then the King, the King himself, cries to Hero, "Keeper of the Chronicle! Light?" And when he turns his face, it is then that Hero sees the mark. A scar new from the burning, a scar like his own—but not like it. It is not the Enchanter's mark, not stamped into the flesh by hot iron. It is like a flower high on the cheekbone, like a crown, like a red and perfect rose. Lifting his hand to his face, Hero discovers that the rough fleshly rim of his own scar has disappeared. The mark of branding has been forever healed.

Overwhelmed, all Hero can do is laugh—the Enchantment truly is broken! And his feet, almost despite themselves, begin to step to the music, and he draws himself up proud, standing tall, a subject of the King, this most beautiful of men *alive*. And he is proud to be called a King's man.

"LIGHT!" he calls back.

The King tosses the dancing fire his way, and Hero's head is bathed in warmth as he feels the wonderful homespun wool of the cloak of Ranger blue falling around his shoulders, and he is lighted through and through. He breathes the sudden cool air of Great Park, fragrant with field and flower. He looks into the eye of street urchin and orphan, and they are truly beautiful. And his soul feels bold; at heart he knows he is a man of courage.

Nearby, Mercie's luxuriant black hair falls to her waist; she is once again the most beautiful of women. Ranger Commander, strong, broad shouldered and grand, bows to his warrior wife. Amanda, in her royal garments, dances in the ring way across the field. Hero watches as the circle moves closer, and he sees the old gladsome laughter in her eyes. He meets her to take her hand and to join the dance beside her as they all, subjects of the Kingdom, laugh and sing and step the sacred steps round and round this Most Royal Highness, His Majesty the King.

It is only then, when the circle is finally fulfilled, and each one he loves has become real with sacred starshine in their eyes, that the King himself turns in motion to the sweet, solemn and glorious music of Great Park.

Then, while his own eyes shine with day, he lifts his hands to the light, and in his first morning of the beginning again of all time, he proclaims aloud, "The Enchantment is broken!

"LET THE RESTORATION BEGIN!"

The young King lives, and so does His dream for the world.

On with the Restoration!

The restoration has begun. The kingdom and kingship will not be complete until our Lord returns in power and glory and rules over the earth. But even now we who are marked by His fire, model for all to see a life of love for God and others. We are the ones who, like "His majesty," treat others the way we would have them treat us.

We say on His behalf, "Are you looking for compassion? For someone to put a loving arm around you as you grieve? Are you searching for the people who will treat you right, according to God's ways? Come, we'll do our best to show you what that looks like."

No one is really inhibiting the church from being the church in this land. That's true in many nations of the world. In Korea, Nigeria, India, Ukraine, Brazil, Australia, Japan, Mexico, even China—it's really difficult to stop believers from acting toward others in a Christlike way if that's what they are determined to do.

In this country, with all its freedoms, there's been a strange twist. It's as if the church here is surprised when our citizenry doesn't adhere to the ways of Christ. In our long history, our society as a whole seldom, if ever, has truly followed Jesus. But I can hardly think of anyplace else in the world where Christians expect citizens or government leaders to do so. It would be wonderful if that happened, but it's hardly the norm. I doubt that Jesus expected Herod to convert. The church, not the government, was to be the light.

Hopefully governments would understand it was to their advantage to have people around who consistently treated others in the way they themselves wanted to be treated.

In America some believers today sound more reactive than

proactive. Rehearsing the bad news rather than living and sharing the Good News, they concentrate on the evils in our society, rather than seeing the increasing opportunities to show "kingslove." This is a barrier we must overcome. A reactive agenda won't capture this generation. Living out Christ's kingdom in their midst is what will win their hearts.

Yes, our society is in bad shape. It's not as bad as some in the world, but even so, all around the globe, often in what would appear to be the most impossible of settings, the kingdom dream lives on and is doing fine. The church is alive with Resurrection fire. The day for spiritual heroics has hardly come to an end. In fact, revival is actually becoming increasingly common. As American believers, let us dare to dream God's dreams again, His dreams for us as individuals and His dreams for the church. It's not too late to dream.

In *Tales of the Resistance,* an hourly cry is often shouted from one watch tower to another. "How goes the world? The world goes not well, but the Kingdom comes!"

In America we need to begin each day with the good news that the young King lives and so does His dream for the world.

Whoever makes the coffee in the morning should call upstairs, "How goes the world?" Whoever hears the question should respond, "The world goes not well, but the kingdom comes."

If you start your day watching "Good Morning America" with Joan Lunden and Charlie Gibson, or "Today" with Bryant Gumbel and Katie Couric, you'll discover that as attractive as these people might be, they don't understand that the world goes not well but the kingdom comes.

Start your day by reading the average newspaper and you'll miss the all-important message of the kingdom.

I find I have to be careful what I read or to whom I listen even in the Christian world. If I pay too much attention to certain sources, I get the impression that the kingdom light went out following the 1992 election. Whatever your thoughts about the young men Clinton and Gore, these leaders aren't keeping the church from being the church. Neither will their administration or any future administration be the real kingdom, or the primary resource for carrying out kingdom objectives.

The young King lives, and His dream for the world lives as well.

Begin each day with this news! Rehearse it again on the morrow. Repeat it daily even as brave brothers and sisters do all around the world. This is a world which goes not well, but the kingdom comes. The enchantment is broken!

Now, on with the restoration!

FOR DISCUSSION AND REFLECTION

1. From your personal experience, would you say the church at large concentrates more on proclaiming good news or on emphasizing bad news?

2. Based on watching religious television, how do you think the average non-Christian would answer the previous question?

3. Reflect on Christ's approach to ministry. Were there obvious evils He chose not to address? Did He primarily preach good news or bad news? Was His ministry proactive or reactive? Be prepared to defend your answer.

4. Without naming the ministry, evaluate an outreach you support finanically or through your prayers. Is it more proactive or reactive?

5. Is it easier for the church to be proactive or reactive? Which is more attractive?

6. On a daily basis, do you tend to be more caught up with bad news than good news? If so, what could you do to balance out your perspective?

READINGS

It's time for the lambs to roar.

What I'm calling for is a radically different way of thinking about our world. Instead of running from it, we need to rush into it. And instead of just hanging around the fringes of our culture, we need to be right smack dab in the middle of it.

Why not believe that one day the most critically acclaimed director in Hollywood could be an active Christian layman in his church? Why not hope that the Pulitzer Prize for investigative reporting could go to a Christian journalist on staff at a major daily newspaper? Is it really too much of a stretch to think that a major exhibit at the Museum of Modern Art could feature the works of an artist on staff at one of our fine Christian colleges? Am I out of my mind to sugest that your son or daughter could be the principle dancer for the Joffrey Ballet Company, leading a weekly Bible study for the other dancers in what was once considered a profession that was morally bankrupt?

I don't think so. In fact, I believe it has been the pessimistic vision of the church that has prevented generations of young people from venturing out into the culture-shaping professions of our world. I've always wondered why we could be so quick to sacrifice our children to become missionaries but stand in the way of their becoming broadcast journalists, film and television actors, photographers, and painters. It's almost as if we believe God is strong enough to take care of his own only as long as they stay within the safety of the Christian ghetto. And yet, the Bible gives us countless examples of people like Joseph, who not only served as an advisor to the "president" of his day but also used that position to influence the entire land.

Can't we do that today? Shouldn't we be encouraging and equipping our sons and daughters to become Josephs too?

A friend of mine told me about a conversation he had with a member of his church. The two were talking about their frustration over their church's inability to have any impact on their community. It was a relatively small church—about 150 members—in an upscale suburban Midwest city. Included in the congregation were a leading surgeon, several business executives, a department head of a prestigious public school, as well as a number of lawyers, teachers, and sales reps. But, my friend observed, we're just sort of treading water. Things are getting worse in our community, families are breaking up, our kids aren't even accepting our faith, and we seem to waste so much time fighting with each other.

My friend then recalled the response of his fellow church member: "Don't you know, Jim, this is as good as it gets."

That church, like so many others, is filled with lambs who've lost their voice. Not only have they failed to penetrate their community with their values, they have come to accept their failure as inevitable.

I believe it's not only possible but absolutely necessary for Christians and Christian values to become a vital element in the overall moral and cultural discourse of our nation. Without our strategic involvement in the culture-shaping arenas of art, entertainment, the media, education, and the like, this nation simply cannot be the great and glorious society it once was. If we are to be obedient to our Lord's call to go into all the world, we will begin reentering the fields that we have fled.

Are you ready to roar?

Roaring Lambs, Bob Briner, Zondervan, pages 31–32.

■ ■ ■

Be still, my soul: thy God doth undertake
To guide the future as He has the past.
Thy hope, thy confidence let nothing shake;
All now mysterious shall be bright at last.
Be still, my soul: the waves and winds still know
His voice who ruled them while He dwelt below.

_____

"Be Still My Soul," by Jean Sibelius.

■　■　■

Christians privileged to live in the last decade before the year 2000 face a historic opportunity.

The number of Christians worldwide is growing at unprecedented rates. A shrinking global village and new technology make it easier to get the message of Christ to those who have never heard. Growing agreement on both the urgency of evangelism and the importance of a holistic approach encourages optimism. And historic political changes have opened more doors to the Gospel. The last decade of the second Christian millennium is a breathtaking time to be a disciple of Jesus Christ.

Global Christianity is on the move. Considerably more people have become Christians in the twentieth century than in any previous century. In 1900, there were about 558 million Christians. In 1992, there were 1,833 million. Experts predict that in eight years—by the year 2000—there will probably be 2,130 million.

One must quickly add that this explosive expansion is almost exactly parallel to the total global population growth. There are also vastly more non-Christians today. In 1900, Christians represented 34.4% of the global population. Christian statistician David Barrettt estimates that Christians will be 34.1 percent in 2000 A.D. There is still much to do.

The ratio of committed Christians to non-Christians, however, offers real hope. Barrett estimates that the number of committed, "Great Commission" Christians is growing at 6.9% a year—more than twice as fast as the total world population. Precise statistics are not available, so one must be careful. But Ralph Winter probably correctly identifies a significant trend when he suggests that in 1950, there were approximately twenty-one non-Christians for every "Bible-believing" Christian. By 1980, he says, there were only eleven non-Christians for every "Bible-believing" Christian. And by 1992, the ratio was less than 7–1.

Pentecostals and charismatics today are the most successful at evangelism, and their numbers are growing at explosive rates. In 1970 there were seventy-two million. Twenty-two years later (1992) they had increased more than 500% to 410 million. Barrett estimates that by the year 2000, Pentecostal and charismatic Christians alone will number 560 million.

The tremendous growth of the church in the Third World is another reason for joy and hope. In 1900 at least 75% of all Christians were white folk living in places like Europe, North America, and Russia. By 2000, 56% of all Christians will be Third World Christians living outside those traditionally "Christian" countries. The number of Christians in Africa, Asia, and Latin America will have increased 1300% in 100 years to almost 1.2 billion people.

It is extremely significant that the number of Third World missionaries is increasing at an astonishing rate. By 1990, there were 49,000 Third World missionaries spreading the Gospel in countries other than their own. By the year 2000, there will probably be 100,000. When one remembers that in 1900, the total number of all foreign missionaries were only 62,000, one can see the magnitude of the huge body of Third World missionaries.

The wonderful privilege of sharing the Gospel cross-culturally with people of a different language and history is no longer a "Western" or "White European" activity. Africans are coming to evangelize in Europe and North America. Native American Navajo Christians are sending missionaries to European Laplanders, and European Gypsies are spreading the Gospel in the African country of Madagascar!

One-Sided Christianity, Ronald J. Sider, Zondervan, pages 187–89.

■ ■ ■

"Ron, the news isn't good. You have leukemia... a slow-moving form of cancer."

He needn't have explained. A pastor friend of mine in Minneapolis had just died of the disease. I knew about leukemia; I just couldn't believe that I had it. It was like someone had grabbed my life's book out of my hands, flipped through the pages, then handed it back to me. And I found myself staring at The Last Chapter—long before I'd ever wanted or expected to. If this was a surprise ending, I didn't want to read it.

Receiving that kind of news is like a punch in the stomach. It knocks the wind out of you. So many things flash through your mind. *Where do I turn? Who do I tell? What should I say? What shouldn't I say?* So many questions. So much confusion. People gather around you to support you in prayer and speak words of faith and hope. Some come with the right remedy at the wrong time. Still others are just plain wrong.

I've heard of every cure under the sun. I have a file full of them. Everything from jumping into a pool with dolphins to bizarre diets to coffee enemas. Some well-meaning people seem to have the clear word from the Lord for me:

"It's just a test of your faith. A pathway to growth."
"Your problem is a lack of faith."
"There is sin in your life."
"You shouldn't be a pastor."
"You're out of the will of God."
"How can you minister to someone who's sick when you need healing yourself?"

During that first barrage of formulas, cures, counsel, and remedies, I remember a very quiet moment when my wife Joyce and I sat together on the couch in our home. I remember her arms around me.

I said, "How are you doing and what do you think?"

She said, "The servant of the Lord is indestructible until God is through with him."

Her words were a strength to me—a comfort when so many things seemed so wrong. We turned to the Lord and His Word, finding particular encouragement and help in the psalms and the Gospels. We were reminded that peace and rest don't come from understanding everything, but from trusting the Lord with all our hearts even when we don't understand anything.

In this the biggest Bad Thing of my life, I was beginning to see some Good Things. The Lord's Mercurochrome was still burning in my wound like fire, but it was *working*.

Surprise Endings, Ron Mehl, Multnomah, pages 15–17.

■ ■ ■

When Michael Korda wrote *Power! How to Get It, How to Use It*, his book quickly became a bestseller. Writing in a provocative, no-nonsense style, the author argued that life is a game of power: getting it, controlling it, and using it to obtain security, fame, sex, and money. After quoting Lord Acton's famous statement that "Power tends to corrupt and absolute power corrupts absolutely," Korda argued that it is worse to not push for power. We live in a world that is run by power, he wrote, and we need to grab it, hang on to it, enjoy it, and use it to get what we want.

Everybody knows about power struggles between husbands and wives, parents and children, rival street gangs, political foes, and opposing factions in universities, corporations, professional organizations, religious denominations, or churches. Most of these struggles involve self-centered actions, hard-feelings, anger, and the manipulation of other people. The players in the power games feel anxiety and insecurity, even when they win the largest share of the power.

It is not easy to be a difference maker in a world, a community, or a family where people are struggling for power. Sometimes, we have to work with individuals (often incompetent and unreasonable individuals) who are jealous of their power and threatened when they learn about our difference-maker plans and passions. At times we must work within the power conscious system of local government. We may have to get approval for our buildings and plans from committees, church boards, or people in positions of power. Sometimes it seems difficult to maintain integrity when we have to live and work in a power-crazed culture. According to futurist Alvin

Toffler, we are entering a period of history when "the entire structure of power that held the world together is now disintegrating." There is a major power shift taking place, says Toffler. It stretches from the highest levels of government to the daily interactions we have with our neighbors, family members, and colleagues at work. As this century ends, it seems that everybody will experience sometimes radical change sin who holds power, how it is used, and how it is controlled."

Despite these changes, however, we are not helpless pawns in the hands of others who hold power or struggle to get it. For centuries, committed and determined difference makers have been able to make significant changes, despite the power of others who get in the way. When God is leading us to make a difference, we can move forward with confidence, especially when we remember two important truths: power can be destructive, but ultimate power belongs to God.

You Can Make a Difference, Gary R. Collins, Zondervan, pages 236–37.